# Environmental Justice

## CONTEXT, CHALLENGES AND NATIONAL APPROACHES

OECD
BETTER POLICIES FOR BETTER LIVES

**Please cite this publication as:**
OECD (2024), *Environmental Justice: Context, Challenges and National Approaches*, OECD Publishing, Paris, https://doi.org/10.1787/57616eb4-en.

ISBN 978-92-64-50983-2 (print)
ISBN 978-92-64-88026-9 (PDF)
ISBN 978-92-64-65907-0 (HTML)
ISBN 978-92-64-42123-3 (epub)

**Photo credits:** Cover image adapted from © Lightspring/Shutterstock.com.

Corrigenda to OECD publications may be found on line at: www.oecd.org/about/publishing/corrigenda.htm.

# Foreword

Environmental justice seeks to redress an array of recurring challenges faced by various communities and groups. These include disproportionate exposure to environmental hazards, unequal access to environmental amenities, and concerns about the uneven implications of environmental policies. These concerns can be exacerbated by the lack of meaningful engagement and legal recourse.

As countries increase their efforts to tackle environmental degradation, pollution and climate change, environmental justice is more relevant than ever as it can shed light on how to ensure fairness in the processes and outcomes of environmental policymaking.

This report examines the plurality of the concept of environmental justice, its underlying conceptual pillars and how it has emerged in different contexts around the world. It also provides the first policy stocktake of how governments across the OECD and beyond are seeking to redress environmental justice concerns, building upon insights from the 26 responses to the OECD Environmental Justice Survey as well as on complementary desk analysis across a broader set of countries.

The report maps the different ways in which environmental justice is pursued whether directly through targeted laws or indirectly through added safeguards for more vulnerable people. Highlighting the variety of levers available to policymakers and exemplifying their practical application across contexts serves to better inform present and future environmental justice efforts.

By showcasing not only common, unifying challenges but also leading approaches, the case for cross-country mutual learning is strengthened. To this end, it is hoped that the insights and practices offered in this report propel advances in environmental justice across OECD countries and beyond.

# Acknowledgements

The report was conceptualised, managed, and edited by Shardul Agrawala, Head of the Environment and Economy Integration Division in the OECD Environment Directorate. All chapters of the report were authored by Julia Kieloch, Edward Bayliss, Yuko Ishibashi, Shardul Agrawala and Nicolina Lamhauge (all OECD Environment Directorate).

This report is an output of the OECD Environmental Policy Committee (EPOC) and its Working Party on Integrating Environmental and Economic Policies (WPIEEP). The Secretariat would like to thank the EPOC and WPIEEP delegates for their feedback on the earlier drafts of this report. The extensive responses to the OECD Environmental Justice Survey from WPIEEP delegates from the OECD member and partner countries are also gratefully acknowledged.

The report builds upon the earlier scoping research by Hélia Costa, Enrico Botta, Kumi Kitamori, Alberto Agnelli, Ioannis Tikoudis, Katherine Hassett and Rose Mba Mébiame. Additional expert inputs were also provided by numerous colleagues: Andrew Brown, Olof Bystrom, Emma DeRoy, Sho Yamasaki, and Shunta Yamaguchi (all OECD Environment Directorate).

Ivan Babiy and Illias Mousse Iye (OECD Environment Directorate) provided administrative support. The report also benefited from support with communication and outreach aspects from Catherine Bremer (OECD Public Affairs and Communications Directorate), Beth Del Bourgo and Emma DeRoy (OECD Environment Directorate). Baseline Arts Ltd. assisted with the design of certain graphic contents of this report. The report also received formatting support from Meral Gedik (independent editor).

# Table of contents

## FIGURES



## TABLES



## BOXES

# Executive summary

**As countries increase their efforts to tackle environmental degradation, pollution and climate change, the concept of environmental justice can shed light on how to ensure fairness in the processes and outcomes of environmental policymaking.** This report examines the plurality of the concept of environmental justice, its underlying conceptual pillars and how it has emerged in different contexts around the world. The report also provides the first policy stocktake of how governments across the OECD and beyond are seeking to redress environmental justice concerns, building upon insights from responses to an OECD Environmental Justice Survey as well as complementary desk analysis across a broader set of countries.

**While no universal definition of environmental justice exists, it seeks to redress an array of recurring challenges faced by various communities and groups**. These challenges include disproportionate exposure to environmental hazards and the subsequent adverse health effects resulting from such exposure, unequal access to environmental amenities, and concerns about the distributional implications of environmental policies. These concerns can be further exacerbated by the lack of meaningful engagement and legal recourse for the affected communities.

**The evolution and manifestation of environmental justice movements are deeply rooted in historical and regional contexts.** Grassroots movements have often raised awareness of environmental justice, as exemplified by protests against illegal dumping of toxic waste in predominantly African American and low income districts in the United States. On the other hand, top-down approaches are also seen in Europe and Latin America through international instruments such as the Aarhus Convention and Escazú Agreement, cementing access to information, participation and justice as “access rights”. The environmental justice movement in South Africa can be traced back to the late 1980s against the backdrop of the broader struggle for democracy. Elsewhere in Africa, concerns about the impact of extractive industries and electronic waste on health and the environment were among the key drivers. The term environmental justice is less common in the Asia-Pacific region, although South Korea has had an explicit focus on it in its environmental policy. In New Zealand, meanwhile, the culturally informed approach to policy recognises the disparate impacts of environmental and climate policy on Indigenous populations.

**Research documenting disproportionate exposure to natural and man-made risks attests to the persisting nature of these concerns.** Examples abound, from immigrants to industrial regions bearing greater environmental burdens, to Indigenous communities disproportionately suffering air pollution caused by increasingly frequent wildfires due to climate change. Compounded by overlooked exposure pathways and uneven adaptive capacity, the disparate quality of the environment can magnify the existing health inequities at the intersection of race, gender, and socioeconomic characteristics. Higher exposure to environmental hazards may further worsen the vulnerability and result in differential health effects. Relatedly, environmental amenities such as green spaces and clean water are also unevenly available to communities. The literature on environmental justice is now also gradually expanding to include differential access to a broader set of environmental amenities, including electric vehicle charging infrastructure.

**There are complex dynamics underpinning inequitable exposure to environmental hazards, which vary across space and over time.** For example, there are instances of racially motivated siting decisions explained in terms of the lower risk of facing community resistance, but firms may also choose to locate their operations based on cost considerations without a discriminatory intent. Over time, the location of facilities and risks can lower the housing costs, inducing socio-economically disadvantaged households to reside in surrounding areas.

**Costs and benefits of environmental policies are also socio-spatially distributed through channels such as labour markets and income effects.** Environmental policies can induce firms to substitute from labour to (labour-saving) technology which disproportionately disadvantages lower-paid workers with less transferrable skills. Protests against the cost impact of environmental policy amidst the interlocking crises of turbulent energy markets and geopolitical tensions further attest to the importance of adequate consideration of distributional impacts in garnering and sustaining public support for ambitious environmental policies.

**An analysis of the responses to the OECD Survey reveals that the term environmental justice is not common among national administrations despite the ubiquity of equity considerations in environmental policy.** From the terminology of "environmental racism" in Canada to "environmental inequalities" in France, alternative or additional terms are used to refer to a similar set of issues. While explicit use of the term signals a more direct approach to tackling persisting and historically salient environmental justice concerns, countries which do not use the term still often address them indirectly by other means.

**Countries deploy different approaches to advance environmental justice.** Direct approaches to environmental justice can entail executive orders or legislation (the United States and South Korea), judicial precedent (Colombia), or policies and initiatives (Germany). Meanwhile, indirect approaches often ground environmental justice in guaranteeing rights such as to the enjoyment of a healthy environment (Croatia) and providing additional protection to vulnerable groups through anti-discrimination law or detailed impact assessments (the United Kingdom). These approaches can be cumulative; more targeted measures can build on rights-based approaches. However, the analysis finds that countries that have purely rights-based approaches consider the substantive aspects of environmental justice in less detail than those with more targeted measures.

**There is widespread focus upon reducing barriers to participation in environmental decision-making.** Although approaches used in practice often focus on the general public, practices of targeted and tailored engagement are emerging, such as having representatives of communities acting as "cultural mediators" to guide consultations with Indigenous communities in Costa Rica or workshops with children to better understand and address their specific needs in Chile. Countries also go beyond making environmental information available, developing locally tailored means for actively delivering information.

**Meanwhile, consideration of disproportionate impacts of environmental policies appears to be an increasingly crucial relative oversight across countries.** While countries do consider distributional implications of environmental policies, the focus tends to be at relatively aggregated levels such as sectoral impacts of climate policies. This underscores the relevance of applying an environmental justice lens to the analysis of differentiated impacts of policies to identify and address less visible impacts and distinct vulnerabilities.

**There are shared challenges underlying the need to address persisting environmental disparities while implementing policy measures for the transition to more environmentally sustainable economies.** Most countries face data, administrative and financial capacity constraints for designing effective policy for protecting vulnerable communities. For instance, the lack of sufficiently granular data can impede the analysis and conceal the true extent of exposure to or adverse health impacts resulting from environmental hazards.

**The variety of approaches and solutions to advance environmental justice suggests there is value in mutual learning to propel progress.** Several approaches, including screening tools and methodologies, are developed in different jurisdictions to consider the multiple facets of vulnerabilities. For instance, impact assessment guidance could be expanded or pre-existing data on environmental quality, geography, and socio-economic indicators could be overlayed. There are already signs of mutual influence, for instance, with the US Environmental Protection Agency's definition cited in the Colombia's judicial ruling. As countries face the unifying objective of tackling environmental challenges as a policy imperative, knowledge gaps can be better addressed through a comparative perspective and sharing of best practice.

# 1 Introduction and overview

While no universal definition of environmental justice exists, it seeks to redress an array of recurring challenges faced by various communities and groups. This chapter introduces these underlying environmental justice challenges which include disproportionate exposure to environmental hazards and the subsequent adverse health effects resulting from such exposure, unequal access to environmental amenities, and concerns about the distributional implications of environmental policies. These concerns can be further exacerbated by the lack of meaningful engagement and legal recourse for the affected communities. This chapter introduces the building blocks of the OECD Environmental Justice Survey, which sought to identify similarities and differences in how countries identify, assess and address environmental justice concerns.

## 1.1. Introduction

There is mounting evidence that, depending on social and economic circumstances, some communities and groups may face disproportionate exposure to environmental hazards, bear an inequitable share of the costs associated with environmental policy and face more barriers to participating in environmental decision-making world (see, for example (Walker, 2012[1]; Mitchell, 2019[2]; Mabon, 2020[3])). The existing literature highlights the links between such disparities and a matrix of demographic and socio-economic variables (Figure 1.1). Environmental justice is about recognising and addressing these issues.

**Figure 1.1. Environmental justice: Dimensions and relevant factors**

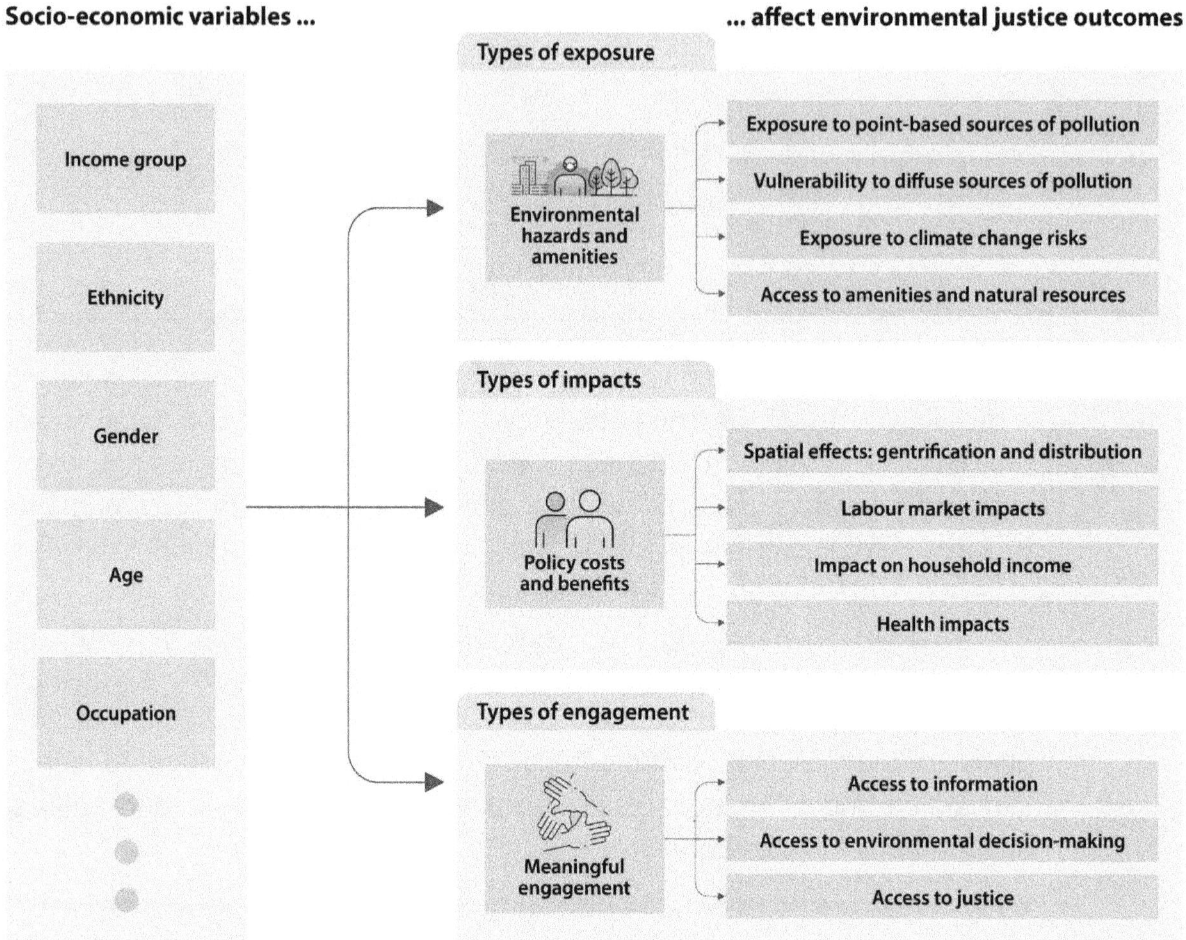


Source: Authors' own elaboration.

An environmental justice lens highlights the linkages between environmental and social conditions. It sheds light on how different levels of environmental quality and protection contribute to the health and wellbeing of some groups, while harming the welfare of others. It also highlights how the environmental goods enjoyed by some groups may come at the expense of those enjoyed by others. Finally, it explores how the ability to influence political change and related decision-making processes varies across groups and communities.

While much of the focus of the literature and policy action is on specific local and national contexts, given the commonality of many of these challenges, an assessment of how environmental justice is advanced in different countries can yield valuable insights and facilitate mutual learning. It is in this context that the OECD has undertaken a cross-country analysis to explore governments approaches to environmental justice. This report aims to shed light on how governments across the OECD and beyond are identifying, analysing, and addressing environmental justice concerns. A survey was distributed to the relevant ministries and agencies of OECD member countries, the European Commission and several non-member countries.[1] Insights from the Survey were complemented by desk research as well as consultations with experts and practitioners.

## 1.2. About the OECD Environmental Justice Survey

The OECD Environmental Justice Survey is exploratory in its aim, seeking to identify the similarities and differences between the approaches to environmental justice across countries. The survey consisted of 20 questions on three key themes: (i) approaches to environmental justice, (ii) assessments and data, (iii) policy measures for environmental justice (Figure 1.2 and Annex A). The first section of the survey explored the approaches countries take to consider environmental justice. Environmental justice was not explicitly defined in the Survey to better explore how the concept is defined and applied in different countries. Instead, the three guiding facets of environmental justice identified (inequitable exposure to environmental hazards and access to environmental amenities, inequitable distribution of the costs and benefits of environmental policy and barriers to access to environmental information, participation in decision-making and legal recourse) were presented to help structure the responses. The section also prompted countries to share what characteristics they consider as relevant when identifying groups and communities at risk. The second section explored the tools and methodologies countries adopt to assess environmental justice concerns. The last section of the survey explored how countries address environmental justice concerns through policies and key challenges they face in their implementation.

### Figure 1.2. Overview of the Survey

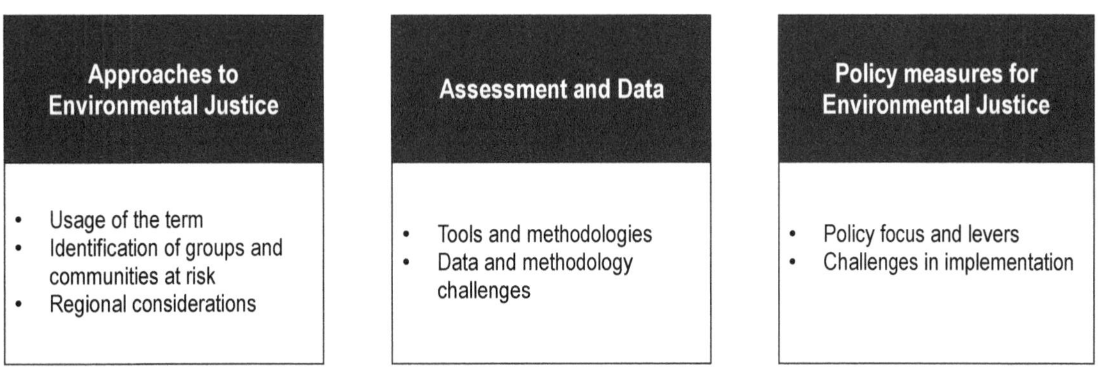


Source: The OECD Environmental Justice Survey

Given the cross-cutting nature of environmental justice issues which may not neatly map onto the remit of ministries and agencies, the Survey encouraged co-ordinated national response to the extent possible. In total, 25 countries (Canada, Chile, Colombia, Costa Rica, Croatia, Estonia, France, Germany, Japan, South Korea, Lithuania, Mexico, New Zealand, Peru, Poland, Portugal, Slovak Republic, South Africa, Spain, Sweden, Switzerland, Türkiye, United Kingdom (where separate responses were received from England and Scotland) and United States) and the European Commission provided response to the Survey. While Environment Ministries were the respondent in the majority of the cases, the responses from some countries were received from multiple ministries and agencies.[2] In the case of the United Kingdom, separate responses were submitted for England and Scotland because the constitutional arrangement of the United Kingdom provides that various environmental powers are devolved to the individual national administrations. However, Northern Ireland and Wales did not respond to the survey. The response from the European Commission represents a regional, rather than a national, approach to environmental justice.[3]

Finally, complementary desk research was also conducted, including for countries like Brazil that have initiatives on environmental justice, but where the survey response was not available. Examples sourced from desk research are therefore marked as such.

## 1.3. Structure of the Report

The remainder of this report is organised as follows. Chapter 2 provides a primer on the diverse ideas environmental justice articulates. It provides an historical account across regions to illustrate the variability of the concept, but also highlights that there are unifying elements and substantive issues that can be usefully studied across different countries to inform policy development. The subsequent two chapters present the main findings from the Survey. Chapter 3 explores the approaches countries take at the national level to consider environmental justice in policymaking. Chapter 4 then turns to how countries identify, assess, and address environmental justice concerns.

## References

Mabon, L. (2020), "Making climate information services accessible to communities: What can we learn from environmental risk communication research?", *Urban Climate*, Vol. 31, https://doi.org/10.1016/j.uclim.2019.100537. [3]

Mitchell, G. (2019), "The messy challenge of environmental justice in the UK: evolution, status and prospects", *Natural England Commissioned Report NECR273*, https://eprints.whiterose.ac.uk/148740/1/2019%20Mitchell%20NE%20EJ%20commissioned%20report%20NECR273.pdf. [2]

Walker, G. (2012), *Environmental Justice: Concepts, Evidence and Politics*, Routledge, London, https://doi.org/10.4324/9780203610671. [1]

## Notes

[1] The survey was sent out to the following countries (countries which provided the response are marked with a *): Argentina, Australia, Austria, Belgium, Brazil, Bulgaria, Canada*, Chile*, Colombia*, Costa Rica*, Croatia*, Czechia, Denmark, Estonia*, Finland, France*, Germany*, Greece, Hungary, Iceland, Indonesia, Ireland, Israel, Italy, Japan*, Korea*, Latvia, Lithuania*, Luxembourg, Mexico*, the Netherlands, New Zealand*, Norway, Peru*, Poland*, Portugal*, Slovak Republic*, Slovenia, South Africa*, Spain*, Sweden*, Switzerland*, Türkiye*, the United Kingdom* and the United States*.

[2] The response from New Zealand was received from Ministry for the Environment and Ministry of Health. The response from Peru was received from a total of 11 Ministries, departments and authorities. The responses from the Directorates under the Ministry of Environment were prioritised for analysis, but the content of this report draws on all responses. The response from Türkiye was received from the government department for which environmental issues typically fall outside of their main remit, namely Small and Medium Enterprises Development Organization.

[3] The response highlighted just transition as the central theme informing policymaking. Details of the response from the European Commission are therefore discussed in areas where just transition and environmental justice concerns may overlap.

# 2 A primer on environmental justice

This chapter draws together various conceptualisations of environmental justice based on a literature review. The chapter traces the evolution of environmental justice around the world, highlighting the ways in which the idea has come to be used by different stakeholders. It then unpacks some substantive issues through which environmental justice concerns can manifest as well as some of their underlying drivers.

Advancing environmental justice begins with recognising how "the environment is socially differentiated and unevenly available" (Walker, 2012, p. 214[1]). It is a plural concept with no universal definition (Debbané and Keil, 2004[2]), encompassing an expansive set of ideas around justice defined in terms of distribution, processes, and recognition (Schlosberg, 2007[3]). As countries increase their efforts to tackle environmental degradation, pollution and climate change, the concept of environmental justice can shed light on how to ensure fairness in the processes and outcomes of environmental policymaking.

## 2.1. Evolution of environmental justice across the world: A brief history

The history of the concept demonstrates that environmental justice has evolved differently across regions (Schlosberg, 2013[4]). The varied focus of policy and scholarship over the decades across countries runs in parallel to the differences in priorities assigned to specific environmental justice concerns and communities. Often facilitated by deliberate efforts of transnational networking among activists, there has been a transfer and diffusion of ideas around environmental justice (Debbané and Keil, 2004[2]). While the concept is often considered to have its roots in the United States, it has become internationalised, with research documenting movements addressing similar concerns across the world (Martinez-Alier et al., 2016[5]) (Box 2.1).

### *2.1.1. North America*

Environmental justice has decades of history dating back to at least the 1980s in the United States, originating from the protests against illegal dumping of toxic waste in predominantly African-American and low-income Warren County in North Carolina (Schlosberg and Collins, 2014[6]). Grassroots movements across the United States and efforts towards evidence gathering[1] helped raise awareness of the disproportionate exposure of ethnic and racial minority and low-income populations to environmental hazards, leading to the US Environmental Protection Agency (EPA) placing environmental justice on its policy agenda. Executive Order 12898[2] followed in 1994, requiring consideration of environmental justice across federal government for the first time (United States Environmental Protection Agency, 2023[7]).[3]

Executive Order 12898 has attracted wider scholarly attention to environmental justice in the United States. While early research focussed on documenting differentiated siting of hazardous waste (Bullard, 1983[8]), the scope gradually expanded to include exposure to other environmental hazards, such as the distribution of air, water and noise pollution (Banzhaf, Ma and Timmins, 2019[9]) as well as varying impact of environmental policies (Shapiro and Walker, 2021[10]). The environmental justice policy agenda has been progressively strengthened over the years, with the EPA now putting it squarely at the centre of its work (OECD, 2023[11]). In 2021, President Joe Biden signed Executive Order 14008 [4] that enhanced the agenda to "advance environmental justice" in efforts to address climate change (White House, 2021[12]). Most recently, Executive Order 14096[5] deepened "the whole-of-government commitment to environmental justice" (White House, 2023[13]).

As the US movement made headlines internationally in 1980s, it prompted the identification of similar patterns of injustice in other countries over time (Mohai, Pellow and Roberts, 2009[14]). In Canada, a recent body of scholarship exploring inequitable distribution of environmental harms, together with environmental justice activism, have propelled environmental justice to feature more prominently in the policy agenda. With research documenting inequitable distribution of environmental harms, including water contamination in Indigenous and Afro-Canadian communities in Nova Scotia (Waldron, 2018[15]) and exposure to mercury among the Grassy Narrows First Nations community (Philibert, Fillion and Mergler, 2020[16]), the severity of disparities in access to a healthy environment has become increasingly recognised. Subsequently, draft legislation to develop a national strategy to "assess, prevent and address environmental racism and to advance environmental justice" is now in motion (Parliament of Canada, 2023[17]).

### 2.1.2. Europe

While the role of grassroots movements is also prominent in Europe, environmental justice has been driven onto the policy agenda in a relatively top-down manner, in response to intergovernmental agreements that seek to advance and uphold human rights (Mitchell, 2019[18]). The Aarhus Convention[6] – establishing rights and duties[7] for ensuring access to information and participation in environmental decision-making – has had an influence on the evolution of the European Union (EU) and informed national governments' legislations and efforts to identify their role (Bell and Carrick, 2017[19]).

In addition, there has also been notable focus on assessments of environmental justice concerns through evidence and data collection and development of indicators in some European countries, with focus on the spatial distribution of health-related environmental burdens and its relation to economic deprivation (Köckler et al., 2017[20]). In the United Kingdom, these efforts resulted in collection of granular neighbourhood data on a range of socio-economic and environmental factors and the creation of an "Index of Multiple Deprivation" (IMD), subsequently informing the development of IMD elsewhere, including Germany (Fairburn, Maier and Braubach, 2016[21]). Recent region-wide evidence also documents uneven exposure to environmental hazards and their health impact, both across and within European countries (European Environment Agency, 2018[22]).

Unlike in North America, there has not been a distinct development of environmental justice as a concept along racial and ethnic backgrounds in Europe. However, the relative lack of evidence highlighting these concerns may also reflect data constraints, since some European countries, including France, prohibit data collection on racial and ethnic origins.[8] Nonetheless, there are some qualitative studies documenting environmental injustice among ethnic minorities in Europe. For instance, against the backdrop of the transition to market economies leading to further geographical isolation of Roma communities in Central and Eastern European countries, wealth of case studies demonstrates that the communities experience inequitable access to environmental amenities and services (Heidegger and Wiese, 2020[23]).

### 2.1.3. Latin America

The development of the environmental justice agenda in Latin American countries coincides with the history of the region's deeper integration into the global economy since the 1990s (Rasmussen and Pinho, 2016[24]). Research in the region has subsequently explored the risks associated with rapid industrial development, such as industrial waste and pollution and their disproportionate impact on low-income groups (Carruthers, 2008[25]). The evolution of how environmental justice has come to be advanced in Mexico is illustrative, with early evidence in 1990s finding disproportionate exposure to chemical hazards in neighbourhoods proximate to industrial parks catered towards exports (*ibid*). Complaints on health impacts by communities and activists eventually led to the co-operation between public agencies in Mexico and the United States, resulting in the commitment to treat industrial wastes in the early 2000s (*ibid*). These cases spotlighted the lack of information and structural mechanisms to address environmental justice concerns, resulting in a series of efforts by governments including enhanced reporting on pollution.

Environmental justice concerns in the region are also compounded by rapid urbanisation and related challenges with providing adequate housing and amenities, leading to the development of informal settlements and slums that are more vulnerable to both natural and man-made environmental hazards (Vásquez et al., 2018[26]). There has also been attention paid to the historical roots of the unequal distribution of land and water resources (*ibid*). For instance, in many parts of Latin America, the notion of autonomy and self-determination among Indigenous communities has acquired an environmental dimension due to the rise of industries, including land use intensive agriculture (Ulloa, 2017[27]).

Notably, an emphasis on regional co-operation towards environmental justice has developed in Latin America over the last decade. The reaffirmed commitment to rights to access to information, participation, and justice (defined in terms of legal recourse) in environmental matters by several Latin American countries at the Rio+20 Summit in 2012 has subsequently led to the conclusion of Escazú Agreement, a regional legal instrument guaranteeing and advancing these rights (Economic Commission for Latin America and the Caribbean, 2022[28]) (Box 2.1). The notion of environmental justice in the region therefore brings participation and access to legal recourse into sharper focus. These developments may reflect, amongst other things, the cross-country nature of major biomes such as the Amazon Rainforest spanning countries, as well as the related concerns over the seeming impunity of those committing environmental crimes and attacks on environmental defenders.[9] For instance, in the third meeting of the Conference of the Parties to the Escazú Agreement, States Parties approved the Action Plan on Human Rights Defenders in Environmental Matter (United Nations, 2024[29]). The Plan highlights priorities and strategic measures to advance the implementation of Article 9 of the Escazú Agreement on human rights defenders in environmental matters.

### *2.1.4. Asia-Pacific*

Unlike many other countries in which environmental justice movements took hold following the catalytic movements in the United States, environmental justice is not a concept commonly referred to in Japan (Fan and Chou, 2017[30]) and Australia (Schlosberg, Rickards and Byrne, 2018[31]). Nonetheless, the term has been used in the broader contexts of studies of environmental pollution during industrial growth in the late 1950s[10] in Japan (Fan and Chou, 2017[30]). The term has also been taken up by Australian Aboriginal communities, whose environmental concerns over natural resources reflect their connection to place and their sense of moral and spiritual obligations to care for "Country"[11] (Schlosberg, Rickards and Byrne, 2018[31]). While the term is also uncommon in New Zealand, the culturally informed approach to policy seeks to recognise the disparate impacts environmental and climate policy might have on Indigenous populations (Ministry for the Environment, 2022[32]).

South Korea is a notable exception in the region, with progressively explicit focus on environmental justice in environmental policy over the last decades. The concept first garnered public attention in 1999, with the Environmental Justice Forum led by environmental activists raising visibility of the issue of unequal access to safe drinking water (Bell, 2014[33]). Greater recognition of the differentiated environmental quality across communities and regions has prompted South Korea to adopt alleviating measures, including through the amendment of the Framework Act on Environmental Policy in 2019.

### *2.1.5. Africa*

In Africa, there has been a notable development on environmental justice in South Africa, which can be traced back to the late 1980s movements against the backdrop of broader struggle for democracy, gaining momentum in the early 1990s (McDonald, 2002[34]). Trade unions and civil society organisations have played a significant role in drawing attention to the failures of the past environmental policies and exposure to toxic waste (Lukey, 2002[35]). Environmental justice entered the popular lexicon in South Africa in the conference organised by Earthlife Africa, one of the key outcomes of which was the establishment of a nation-wide organisation that coordinated activities of environmental and social justice activists (McDonald, 2002[34]). The recognition of environmental rights, including with respect to access to participation followed in the 1994 Bill of Rights, later adopted in the new Constitution in 1996 (Hall and Lukey, 2023[36]).

Much of the environmental justice research in Africa has been anchored in the context of economic development, elucidating linkages between hazards posed by certain industries and their simultaneous centrality to their national economies. Particular attention is paid to the impact of extractive industries (Aldinger, 2013[37]; Banza et al., 2009[38]; Martinez-Alier, 2001[39]) or electronic waste (Akese and Little, 2018[40]) on human health and the environment. Some also highlight that the scope of environmental justice might be in fact broader in sub-Saharan Africa than often envisaged in other countries, reflecting the unique nature of rural communities' relationship with land and their reliance on natural resources (Aldinger, 2013[37]).

**Box 2.1. Documenting environmental justice concerns around the world: The Global Environmental Justice Atlas (EJAtlas)**

The environmental justice movement has been described as "locally embedded but globally connected" (Cock, 2006, p. 22[41]). An illustrative outcome of the deliberate transnational networking of environmental justice activism is the Environmental Justice Atlas (EJAtlas), created in 2014. The EJAtlas is an interactive online archive, documenting and cataloguing cases of socio-environmental conflicts around the world (Global Environmental Justice Atlas, 2024[42]). Exemplifying the evolution of environmental justice as activism and a field of research, it is maintained by collaborators across countries including civil society organisations and academics.

The EJAtlas provides visibility to the instances of environmental justice concerns that may otherwise remain unrecognised (Martinez-Alier et al., 2016[5]). While each documented incidence reflects local grievances, it draws attention to the prevalence of environmental justice concerns around the world. Over the last 50 years, over 3300 cases have been documented (Global Environmental Justice Atlas, 2024[42]).

## 2.2. Key conceptual pillars of environmental justice and related concepts

As the history across regions demonstrates, the concept of environmental justice articulates a diverse set of ideas, and there is currently no universal definition or metric to measure environmental justice (Walker, 2012[1]). Different ways in which environmental justice concerns manifest can limit the extent to which the concept can be defined in a way that is useful across countries. However, there are recurrent elements that can be considered as key conceptual pillars of environmental justice:(i) distributive, (ii) procedural and (iii) recognitional justice (Schlosberg, 2004[43]).

### *2.2.1. Distributive justice*

Reflecting the historical origins rooted in activism that raised visibility of environmental inequities, distributional considerations are often at the heart of environmental justice. Distributive justice draws attention to the need to consider how the multiple patterns of existing inequities based on characteristics of communities might result in inequitable exposure, vulnerability to environmental hazards and inability to access environmental amenities, as well as the differentiated impact policies can have on communities.

### *2.2.2. Procedural justice*

Environmental justice also highlights the importance of processes and procedures, recognising the need to understand how decisions are made, who can be involved and influence environmental decisions. Procedural justice can be understood both as a means to correct for inequitable distribution as well as an end in itself for achieving environmental justice (Bell and Carrick, 2017[19]). Reflecting this dual importance, environmental justice movements often call for various formats of participation that are attuned to the diversity of the communities (e.g. cultural and linguistic) to enable their meaningful participation in environmental decision-making (Schlosberg, 2004[43]). The fundamental importance of meaningful participation in environmental decision-making and access to information as human rights is also highlighted in various international and regional instruments (Box 2.2).

### *2.2.3. Recognitional justice*

Recognitional justice identifies the disrespect and systematic undervaluation of certain communities as a source of injustice (Whyte, 2017[44]). Lack of recognition may arise from the failure to acknowledge the varying environmental and cultural identities and heritages (Schlosberg, 2004[43]; Fraser, 2000[45]). Recognitional justice is often discussed in the contexts of racialised minorities and Indigenous Peoples, but it is an encompassing concept that cautions against systemic and excessive generalisation of groups and communities (Whyte, 2017[44]).[12] Respecting the diverse values and experiences of communities is therefore seen as an antecedent condition for attaining distributional and procedural justice. Figure 2.1 describes the complex interlinkages that demonstrate how these three pillars of (in)justice can reinforce each other.

**Figure 2.1. Interlinkages of distributive, procedural and recognitional environmental (in)justice**

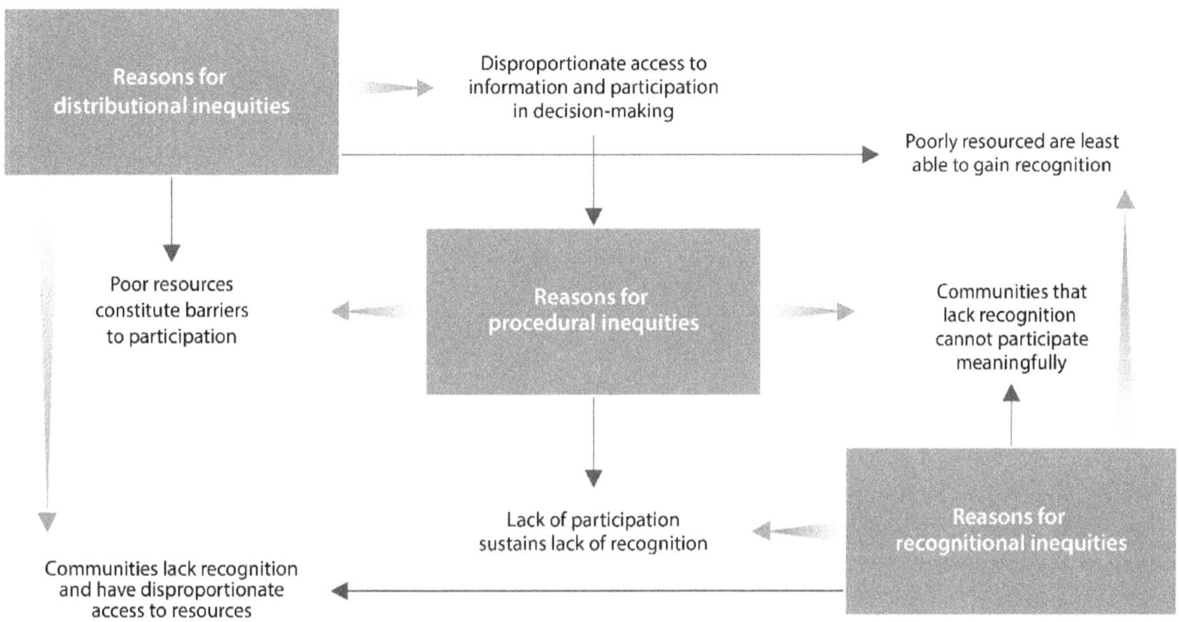


Source: Adapted from (Walker, 2012, p. 65[1])

**Box 2.2. Role of international instruments in advancing procedural environmental justice**

**The Convention on Access to Information, Public Participation in Decision-Making and Access to Justice in Environmental Matters (Aarhus Convention), 1998**

While the Convention does not explicitly refer to environmental justice, it obliges Parties to guarantee access rights to information, participation in decision-making and justice with the objective "to contribute to the protection of the right of every person of present and future generations to live in an environment adequate to his or her health and well-being" (UNECE, 1998[46]). In the European Union, these obligations have been translated into European law through directives that are directly applicable in all EU member states through the Access to Environmental Information Directive (2003/4/EC) and the Public Participation Directive (2003/35/EC) (European Commission, n.d.[47]).

**The Regional Agreement on Access to Information, Public Participation and Justice in Environmental Matters in Latin America and the Caribbean, also known as the Escazú Agreement, 2018**

With a similar focus on procedural rights, the Escazú Agreement is an instrument aimed at both environmental and human rights protection (Economic Commission for Latin America and the Caribbean, 2018[48]). The Agreement places a significant emphasis on individual and groups in vulnerable situations and includes special provisions for protecting their rights to information, participation and justice. Individuals and groups in vulnerable situations are also defined in Article 2 (e) of the agreement: "Persons or groups in vulnerable situations" means those persons or groups that face particular difficulties in fully exercising the access rights recognized in the present Agreement, because of circumstances or conditions identified within each Party's national context and in accordance with its international obligations" (*ibid*). It has been ratified by 16 countries, which renders it a key instrument for advancing environmental justice in the regions. Parties to the Escazú Agreement operationalise the principles specified individually.

**Common principles and regional specificities**

The Aarhus Convention and the Escazú Agreement, although two decades apart in their respective adoption, are both important elaborations of the Principle 10 of the Rio Declaration (Barritt, 2020[49]), which notes "environmental issues are best handled with participation of all concerned citizens, at relevant level" (United Nations, 1992[50]). However, there are important differences, reflecting the regionally differentiated expressions of the seemingly universal values of promoting access rights (Barritt, 2020[49]). For instance, Escazú Agreement is the first international agreement that contains provisions (Article 9) to improve protection for environmental defenders (Andrade-Goffe, Excell and Sanhueza, 2023[51]).

### *2.2.4. Environmental justice and related concepts*

Reflecting the expansion of the environmental justice discourse across space and over time, the concepts with "justice" or "just" appellations have expanded over the last decade (Agyeman et al., 2016[52]). In particular, the concept of "climate justice" has gained currency in policy discourse in recent years. The origin of the term climate justice is intricately linked to the evolution of environmental justice (Schlosberg and Collins, 2014[6]). Climate change has a significant distributive dimension, both in its causes and effects, as evidenced by the highly uneven nature of emissions across and within countries (Bruckner et al., 2022[53])[13] and the burdens borne by those least responsible for historical emissions (Agyeman, Bullard and Evans, 2002[54]). It is also routinely deployed by an array of stakeholders to mobilise action and to discuss loss and damage, historical responsibility as well as the distribution of financing and adaptation needs (Wang and Lo, 2021[55]), particularly in low-income countries (Resnik, 2022[56]). Climate justice is also rooted in intergenerational justice, problematising the inadequate consideration given to the welfare of children, youth and the future generations (Gibbons, 2014[57]).

"Just transition" is another term that has acquired prominence as distributive consequences of the transition to more environmentally sustainable economies become increasingly visible. Recognising the opportunities and challenges that come with the scale of economic and social transformation needed to address pressing environmental challenges, including climate change, it draws attention to the need to ensure that no one is left behind and for policies to compensate for the disruptive impact of the transition (Intergovernmental Panel on Climate Change, 2023[58]). Originally a labour-oriented term[14] deployed by trade unions in 1980s to advocate for greater protection for workers who faced the prospect of unemployment due to policy-induced economic restructuring, it has broadened to encompass multiple social and economic transitional impacts including energy access (Wang and Lo, 2021[55]). The concept has gained recognition as a guiding approach to policy design and implementation, building on the widespread international endorsement of the "Guidelines for a just transition towards environmentally sustainable economies and societies for all" (International Labour Organization, 2016[59]).

There are considerable ambiguities in how environmental justice, climate justice and just transition are defined and used in policy discussions. Nonetheless, they are often construed with a shared emphasis on equity and fairness, reflecting their origins and mutual influence. In addition, they all highlight the distinct vulnerability of some communities, bringing attention to the disproportionality of burdens and the importance of distributive and procedural considerations (McCauley and Heffron, 2018[60]).

While environmental justice scholarship is often associated with site- and community-specific impact (Rasmussen and Pinho, 2016[24]), there are important national and regional dimensions. Similarly, while climate justice is commonly associated with international implications of climate change, uneven impact of climate change and the adaptation needs manifest at local, regional and national scales (Schlosberg and Collins, 2014[6]). For instance, low-income groups in developing countries can be more vulnerable to climate change than higher income groups in those countries, due to skewed investments in disaster risk reduction in affluent areas[15] and lower housing and land prices leading to their disproportionate settlements in risk-prone areas (Hallegatte et al., 2020[61]). The concept of just transition, meanwhile, highlights the varied sectoral impact of the transition to more environmentally sustainable economies, but it is also multiscale insofar as the social and economic transformation necessitated by the transition also brings national and international implications (McCauley and Heffron, 2018[60]).

Another distinction can be made on the temporal dimension. Some scholars consider that, although environmental justice and climate justice both weave together the lasting consequences of injustices from the past and the pressing need to address the distributive concerns of the present, climate justice and just transition also entail a distinct focus on future trajectories (Jenkins, 2018[62]). Despite these notable overlaps in theory and practice, these concepts also serve distinct and equally important purpose of framing policy discussions and informing policy design.

## 2.3. Unpacking the substantive issues of environmental justice

The context-specific nature of evidence on environmental injustice defies generalisation across different countries. For instance, while environmental justice research finds low-income groups tend to experience inequitable environmental outcomes, the characterisation of these groups as universally disadvantaged may not always hold as there are local nuances as well as important exceptions (Hajat, Hsia and O'Neill, 2015[63]).

However, decades of interdisciplinary research have shown that there are also certain commonalities among environmental justice concerns across space and time, which include the following three key substantive issues: (i) inequitable exposure to environmental hazards and access to environmental amenities, (ii) inequitable distribution of the costs and benefits of environmental policy, and (iii) barriers to access environmental information, participation in decision-making and legal recourse. The characteristics of the disproportionately affected segments of the population and the extent to which specific issues are considered problematic necessarily differ across countries. It is also important to note that these three substantive issues are not exhaustive; rather they are recurring issues which have implications for environmental justice and for health outcomes in affected populations. Nonetheless, the salience of these issues suggests that there is a scope for mutual learning in terms of how governments can identify, analyse and address these concerns.

### 2.3.1. Inequitable exposure to environmental hazards and access to environmental amenities

Research on environmental justice has long documented the inequitable distribution and exposure to both natural and man-made environmental risks. These can entail exposure to: (i) point source pollution (e.g. toxic chemical release from industrial facilities), (ii) non-point source pollution (e.g. water contamination from agricultural runoff) and (iii) natural hazards (e.g. flooding). While some of the contaminants have established and recognised exposure pathways, there are other pathways, as well as the uneven availability of coping mechanisms that are often given little attention or poorly understood. Furthermore, recent research has also expanded the scope of inquiry to consider differential access to environmental amenities which may exacerbate existing vulnerabilities.

These inequities can also increase risks of adverse health and welfare outcomes of communities already overburdened by pollution. With evidence establishing the links between health and contaminants such as air pollution – the most significant environmental cause of mortality (Manisalidis et al., 2020[64]) – inequitable exposure can interact with other social determinants of health[16] and individual vulnerabilities, translating into further exacerbation of inequitable health outcomes.

*Types of pollution and unevenly available adaptive mechanisms*

**Point source pollution**

Reflecting the historical origin of the environmental justice movement, and in part the ubiquity of waste production in modern life, evidence describing inequities in exposure to environmental hazards is particularly rich on hazardous waste and related air, water and land pollution around the world (Walker, 2012[1]). While early research has focussed on the relation between race and income and siting of facilities such as hazardous waste landfills (Been, 1994[65]) and incinerators (Bullard, 1990[66]; Bullard, 1983[8]) in the United States, the scholarship has also expanded over the decades to include an array of point source pollution as well as the impact of a broader matrix of socio-economic factors and geographic characteristics (Sze and London, 2008[67]). For instance, there is now evidence highlighting a host of concerns over environmental burdens placed on immigrants in industrial regions (Viel et al., 2011[68]), rural communities living in proximity to industrial livestock operations (Kravchenko et al., 2018[69]), as well as on the localised effects of transnational activities (Box 2.4).

While there are continued discussions as to why inequitable exposure arises (Box 2.4), there have been some methodological advances in identifying the inequitable exposure to these point source pollution, allowing a shift away from the focus on "unit-hazard coincidence" that compares the demographic makeup of the geographical units that contain hazards (which problematically disregards the exposure of nearby communities just outside of the chosen unit) and measurement of the distance to pollution sources (Banzhaf, Ma and Timmins, 2019[70]). While proximity to sources of pollution continues to be fundamental to understanding the inequitable exposure, more nuanced methodologies incorporate the different physical and chemical properties of pollutants and their dispersion patterns (Cain et al., 2023[71]).

**Non-point source pollution**

In contrast to point source pollution, non-point source pollution (NPS, also known as diffuse pollution) occurs from multiple pollutants and heterogeneous sources (e.g. households, agricultural runoff) to which individual units of emissions often cannot accurately be attributed (Xepapadeas, 2011[72]).[17] The distribution of the impact of water pollution can put disproportionate burden on some communities, reflecting the interconnectedness of water systems. For instance, watersheds[18] can act as a conduit for both point and NPS pollution, transferring the costs of upstream pollution onto communities with fewer resources at the end of the watershed (Finewood et al., 2023[73]). Due to the difficulty in attributing the cause of ground and surface water NPS pollution to heterogeneous actors and high transaction costs of coordination (OECD, 2012[74]), it can be challenging to redress inequitable exposure, which manifests in the uneven availability of safe and affordable drinking water (Karasaki et al., 2023[75]).

## Box 2.3. Transnational Environmental Considerations

International trade and the transnational context in which businesses operate can be relevant considerations in domestic environmental policy making. Environmental justice scholarship has also brought attention to, for instance, trade in toxic waste and material extraction in relation to global economic inequalities, using the term "unequal ecological exchange" (Pellow, 2008[76]; Martinez-Alier, 2001[39]). While relatively nascent, there is a body of research considering the local environmental (e.g. water and energy) and social impact of the rapidly developing import-oriented strategies for the expanding the use of hydrogen produced from renewables (Müller, Tunn and Kalt, 2022[77]; Dillman and Heinonen, 2022[78]).

### International trade and environmental effects

International trade has conferred innumerable welfare and economic benefits, lifting millions of people out of poverty and providing means and opportunities for sustaining livelihoods across countries (World Bank Group and World Trade Organization, 2015[79]). However, although trade can contribute to environmental sustainability, for instance, by enabling the transfer of clean technologies (Garsous and Worack, 2021[80]), there have also been concerns over its overall environmental impact. Recognising the opportunities and challenges of promoting open trade while mitigating their negative impact, countries have put in place mechanisms to embed environmental considerations in their trade agreements. Examples include the "single entry point", a public submission mechanism applicable to all EU free trade agreements, through which the public can lodge complaints against breaches of sustainability commitments (European Commission, n.d.[81]). Relatedly, many countries increasingly include environmental provisions in their Regional Trade Agreements (RTAs) negotiated between trade partners (OECD, 2023[82]).

### Role of corporations

The environmental justice movement has also long recognised the impacts of the activities of corporations (Foerster, 2019[83]), with the movements in the United States in the 1990s highlighting the responsibility of multi-national enterprises. Such concerns remain relevant as environmental justice concerns persist, for example, in the context of resource extraction, waste disposal (Martínez Alier, 2020[84]) and chemical safety. The EJAtlas (see also Box 2.2) identifies more than a thousand disputes between communities and corporations (Global Environmental Justice Atlas, 2024[42]).

For instance, the Bhopal gas disaster in India 40 years ago – which occurred during Union Carbide's operations – killed thousands of people, permanently injured hundreds of thousands more, and is widely regarded as the most grievous chemical industrial disaster to date (Eckerman and Børsen, 2021[85]). Despite dwindling publicity of Bhopal's aftermath, its socio-economic and environmental legacy endures: females continue to be afflicted by reproductive health problems, children continue to suffer cognitive disabilities, chronic illnesses are widespread, and water and soil remain contaminated (Deb, 2023[86]). There is also evidence of long-term employment effects as those who were in-utero at the time of the disaster are more likely to have a disability that affected their employment, have higher cancer rates, and lower educational attainment (McCord et al., 2023[87]).

These tragedies, and their long-term repercussions, demonstrate the critical impact corporate activities can have upon society, the economy, and the environment. At the same time, these issues highlight the importance on considering how business community, regardless of its size and where it operates, can assume a more active role in preventing adverse impact to the environment. In this context, the OECD Due Diligence Guidance for Responsible Business Conduct provides principles and practical actions to identify, prevent and mitigate the adverse impacts of their operations, supply chains and other business relations, while recognising and promoting the positive contributions of businesses (OECD, 2018[88]).

### Natural hazards and climate change

As the impact of climate change becomes increasingly visible, research has also brought attention to the inequitable distribution of environmental risks (Collins and Grineski, 2018[89]). As devastating events such as Hurricane Katrina in 2005 vividly demonstrate, natural hazards affect communities differently over their entire cycle, from initial impact, evacuation, and post-disaster recovery (Bullard and Wright, 2018[90]). A large body of studies has documented disproportionate impact of natural hazards across communities and individuals. For instance, there is research evidencing the uneven long-term exposure to wildfire-induced air pollution for Indigenous communities (Casey et al., 2024[91]), as well as the significantly higher mortality rate of the people with disabilities during natural disasters (Stein and Stein, 2022[92]).[19] However, the fact that the proximity to risk-prone neighbourhoods brings both environmental risks and amenities (e.g. access to sea and river) defies simplistic characterisation of vulnerabilities in terms of spatial dimension (Collins and Grineski, 2018[89]).

Importantly, interlinkages between man-made environmental risks and climate risks are increasingly recognised. Industrial accidents triggered by disruptive extreme weather events are becoming a greater concern, exposing surrounding communities to acute risks (Johnston and Cushing, 2020[93]). Even after closure of industrial facilities, water and soil contaminants from legacy facilities can still be redistributed by flooding and hurricane, giving rise to new inequities at the intersection of legacy pollution and the increase in the severity and frequency of natural hazards (Marlow, Elliott and Frickel, 2022[94]). These concerns attest to the growing challenge of rectifying persisting issues from the past while mitigating the anticipated climate impact in the future.

### Unevenly available adaptive mechanisms

Compounding inequitable exposure, financial constraints can prevent vulnerable communities from adapting to pollutants and hazards by relocating or purchasing mitigating products or technologies (Ezell et al., 2021[95]; Boyd, 2023[96]). Adaptive mechanisms to unsafe drinking water, for instance, incur additional financial burdens from buying bottled water and investing in costly filtering system – choices that may be unavailable to low-income groups – as well as psychological distress (Karasaki et al., 2023[75]). Another example is the financial constraints to adapt and cope with climate impact such as increasingly frequent heat waves, with some research finding that energy expenditure is less responsive to extreme temperature in low-income households, suggesting the differential adaptive capacity (Doremus, Jacqz and Johnston, 2022[97]).

Even when policy measures are available to remedy inequitable exposure, empirical research suggests that vulnerable communities' take up and participation can be hindered by various barriers in practice. In the case of lead service line inspection and replacement programme for safe drinking water in the United States, various non-financial barriers including lack of trust in water systems, lack of knowledge and inconvenience of scheduling appointments hindered participation in the programme (Klemick et al., 2024[98]). Financial barriers can also limit participation, particularly in less affluent areas in which cost burdens fall on users due to the utility providers' inability to access credits and public funds, making participation cost prohibitive for many low-income groups (Klemick et al., 2024[98]; Allaire and Acquah, 2022[99]).

## Box 2.4. Mechanisms underlying disproportionate burden and proximity to sources of environmental hazards

While observational studies documenting the linkages between environmental and social outcomes help draw attention to environmental justice concerns, evidence exploring why they occur is relatively limited (Knoble and Yu, 2023[100]). Establishing and explaining causality has proved challenging, particularly as the mobility of people and their choices in residential location necessitates longitudinal analysis that capture the demographic makeup before and after the siting decision (Mohai and Saha, 2015[101]).

Existing research has reached diverse conclusions (Mohai, Pellow and Roberts, 2009[14]). Some inequitable exposure to hazardous waste may arise, for example, because of discriminatory intent of siting decisions of facilities. For instance, (Bullard, 1990[66]) has found that siting of hazardous facilities was motivated by racial discrimination against African American communities in the United States. Relatedly, decisions can reflect sociopolitical considerations, with firms selecting "path of least resistance" where communities are least equipped to mobilise action towards opposition (Collins, Munoz and Jaja, 2016[102]). However, studies have also found that firms make their initial siting choices based on conventional economic costs, including access to low-cost labour and land (Wolverton, 2009[103]). Nonetheless, even when the decisions are not intentionally discriminatory, they can still disproportionately affect socio-economically disadvantaged communities over time through market dynamics by lowering the land and property value of the surrounding areas (Mohai, Pellow and Roberts, 2009[14]). These dynamics driving firm and residential sorting are also likely to interact (Cain et al., 2023[71]).

The various drivers behind why some communities are overrepresented in areas in proximity to hazards suggests that these inequities need to be assessed at multiple scales and over time, with involvement of affected communities; otherwise, their broad generalisation can mask particular vulnerabilities and reinforce their lack of recognition (Walker, 2012[1]).

### Environmental amenities

Emerging literature also extends the discussion to access to environmental amenities (Agyeman et al., 2016[52]), such as green spaces, which can promote positive physical and mental health (James et al., 2015[104]). It can also attenuate harm from runoff, extreme temperature, and air pollution (Franchini and Mannucci, 2018[105]). There is substantial evidence suggesting that the access to environmental amenities is also highly uneven (Watkins and Gerrish, 2018[106]). In particular, there is a wealth of studies highlighting the inequitable access to green and blue space in urban areas. Research finds that socio-economic factors and characteristics – including income, race and education – influence access to (Dai, 2011[107]) and quality of the green (Fossa et al., 2023[108]) and blue space (Thornhill et al., 2022[109]). It is also important to highlight that the value communities assign to environmental amenities are relative, and the unmet needs can also raise concerns over environmental justice (Walker, 2012[1]).

There is a growing recognition that there is more to environmental amenities beyond the enjoyment and access to clean and safe natural environment, with some conceptualisation broadening the notion to consider the built environment such as uneven access to electric vehicles (EVs) charging infrastructure. For instance, inequitable access can arise along two dimensions of affordability and ownership of EVs and accessibility of charging infrastructure, which can become self-perpetuating as uneven uptake of EVs may result in differential investments into the infrastructure (Hopkins et al., 2023[110]).

### *Exposure pathways and their environmental justice implications*

Many toxic contaminants have relatively established exposure pathways, depicting a route from sources of pollution and their receptor population (Burger and Gochfeld, 2011[111]). However, some of the atypical pathways can be inadvertently overlooked in exposure science and environmental epidemiology, hindering proactive policy response. These exposure pathways could relate to cultural and religious practice of Indigenous communities including the use of certain medicines and traditional lifestyles centred around outdoors activities and diet (*ibid*). For example, studies from Brazil and Canada found that Indigenous Peoples whose diet is traditionally rich in fish and marine mammal meat were more exposed to mercury poisoning (Chan and Receveur, 2000[112]; Hacon et al., 2020[113]).

Another oft-overlooked exposure pathway is consumption of packaged and canned food and the use of consumer products. For instance, low-income groups might be disproportionately exposed to chemicals[20] used in food packaging for more affordable processed food, as well as canned food with long shelf lives used for food assistance (Ruiz et al., 2018[114]). Research has also examined the exposure pathways through consumer products, such as personal care products that disproportionately affect women and intersect with other categories including race[21] (Zota and Shamasunder, 2017[115]; Collins et al., 2023[116]). More broadly, an exposure pathway can also be structured by the differential indoor environment, such as size and quality of dwellings, which mediates the outdoor and the indoor environment and influences exposure to air and lead pollution (Adamkiewicz et al., 2011[117]); an important consideration given that people globally spend around 85-90% of their lifespan in indoor spaces (Mannan and Al-Ghamdi, 2021[118]).

Furthermore, there is growing evidence of the relation between occupation and additional exposure pathways. For instance, informal waste collectors resorting to burning of plastics in open pits due to lack of waste management facilities are exposed to health threatening dioxin (United Nations Environment Programme, 2021[119]). Furthermore, "take-home" exposure pathways through which workers bring residues on their clothes, shoes and skin into home can expose other members of the households to toxic contaminants (Hyland and Laribi, 2017[120]). Children are particularly more exposed due to physiological and behavioural susceptibility including the propensity to spend more time on the ground where dust-borne residues settle (*ibid*).

Limited data availability and lack of visibility can hinder identification of these exposure pathways. Monitoring can also be hindered due to high costs for installation and maintenance of new devices and inadequate data collection, potentially concealing true extent of pollution (United States Environmental Protection Agency, 2023[121]). In this context, the term "popular epidemiology" has been coined to suggest that lay knowledge and lived experience of exposure to toxic pollution can lead to identify hitherto unacknowledged exposure pathways (Brown, 1997[122]). Active engagement with concerned communities, for instance, through citizen science,[22] helps access local expert knowledge of the communities (Brulle and Pellow, 2006[123]) and elucidate overlooked linkages between the environment and health (Johnston and Cushing, 2020[93]). For example, in Ecuador, a popular epidemiology study conducted in cooperation with rural and Indigenous communities helped establish the links between oil contamination in the region and adverse health impacts, evidence of which was used in legal proceedings against the corporation responsible for the oil extraction (San Sebastián and Hurtig, 2005[124]). They can also complement the traditional environmental monitoring.

### *Environmental justice and health*

There is a widespread recognition that declining environmental quality adversely affects health outcomes. It is estimated that modifiable environmental risk factors have accounted for almost quarter of deaths worldwide in 2012 (WHO, 2016[125]). In particular, there is mounting evidence documenting air pollution and its links to non-communicable diseases, particularly cardiovascular and respiratory diseases (Prüss-Ustün et al., 2019[126]). Importantly, differential exposure, lack of viable options for adaptation, and unacknowledged pathways interact with other socio-economic determinants of health, which can together exacerbate existing health inequities.[23]

Available evidence corroborates the links between the differential availability and quality of the environment and inequitable health outcomes to a wide range of socio-economic variables and categories including income, race, Indigeneity, age and sex. For instance, exposure to environmental hazards can contribute to short-term and long-term maternal health impacts (e.g. miscarriage, higher risk of breast cancer) (Boyles et al., 2021[127]). Disadvantaged women might thus face a "double jeopardy" posed by chronic stressors and exposure to environmental hazards (Morello-Frosch and Shenassa, 2006[128]). Exposure to environmental hazards can also have different impacts for different age groups. For example, children are known to be more susceptible to negative health outcomes of such an exposure due to their biological vulnerabilities (e.g. greater consumption of toxins relative to body weight, immature metabolic pathways) and age-related exposure patterns (e.g. playing close to the floor and the ground and hand-to-mouth behaviours) (Landrigan, Rauh and Galvez, 2010[129]).

Exposure to environmental harms alone is rarely the sole determinant of adverse health outcomes (United States Environmental Protection Agency, 2023[130]). Holistically and accurately attributing the impact of the environmental hazards to health therefore requires careful consideration of other determinants of the impact of the environment on health. Intrinsic factors, biological traits and pre-existing health conditions make some individuals more susceptible to environmental risks. For instance, exposure to environmental hazards, notably air pollution, can exacerbate asthma symptoms. Consequently, environmental exposure is estimated to account for 44% of asthma's disease burden (WHO, 2016[125]).[24]

Importantly, socioeconomic characteristics of individuals, community and health outcomes interact in a multitude of complex and cumulative ways, with research demonstrating that different types of environmental harms tend to cluster in the same community (Banzhaf, Ma and Timmins, 2019[9]) (Figure 2.2).[25] For instance, poor residential condition of low-income groups and exposure to indoor pollution can lead to risks to compromised respiratory systems, which in turn makes them more vulnerable to outdoor air pollution (Solomon et al., 2016[131]). Other variables linked to socio-economic status, such as location of their residence exposed to higher traffic emissions from mobile sources (e.g. vehicles) and inability to move out of the area due to financial constraints, further disproportionately expose communities living in the area to greater level of air pollution to the detriment of their health (Barnes, Chatterton and Longhurst, 2019[132]; Park and Kwan, 2020[133]).

The concept of "exposome", encompassing life-course environmental exposures from prenatal period can help uncover these linkages, distinguishing between individual health characteristics, specific external (e.g. environmental pollutants and chemical contaminants) and general external (e.g. social determinants of health) environment over life course (Wild, 2012[134]). Lifetime cumulative impacts is important to consider given the inequities at birth or in-utero can have lasting consequences for welfare and gaps in opportunities between children based on family backgrounds (Currie, 2011[135]). However, the dynamic nature of exposome and the number of significant challenges that make holistic assessments time-and data-intensive, due to the need to deploy of multiple tools, technologies and large sample sizes to disentangle the different correlated exposures and their interactions (Siroux, Agier and Slama, 2016[136]).

**Figure 2.2. Interactions of socio-economic variables, environment and health**

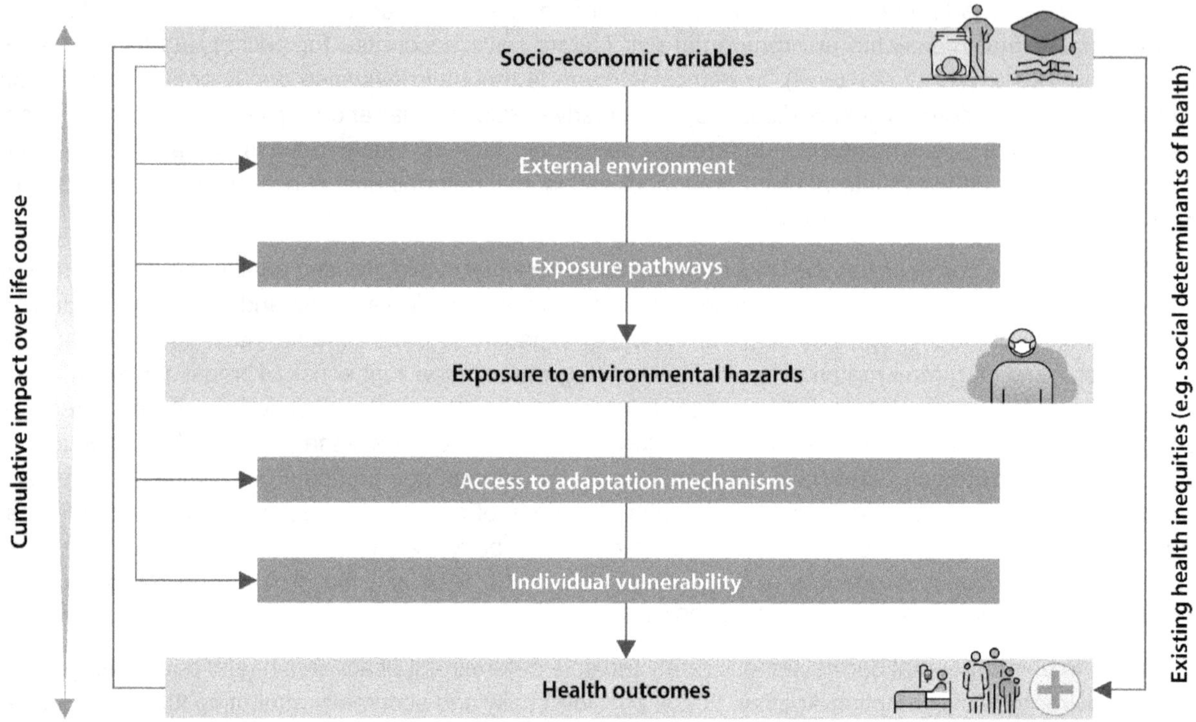


Source: Adapted from (Wakefield and Baxter, 2010[137]) with authors' edits based on (Siroux, Agier and Slama, 2016[136]) and (Burger and Gochfeld, 2011[111]).

### *2.3.2. Inequitable distribution of the costs and benefits of environmental policy*

Another key substantive issue is inequitable distribution of the costs and benefits of environmental policy. While it may seem intuitive that environmental improvements would benefit society at large, empirical literature points to the critical importance of considering the costs of policies. Similarly, improvements in overall environmental quality do not necessarily guarantee that the benefits are enjoyed by all segments of the population (Mitchell, 2019[18]) or that the relative gaps in environmental quality experienced are narrowed; indeed, a recent study suggests that while air quality has improved overall in the United States, the gap between the most and least polluted areas remain relatively stable (Colmer et al., 2020[138]). The inequitable distribution of costs and benefits of policies might be additionally exacerbated by insufficient monitoring and enforcement efforts, potentially causing disparities in compliance with environmental regulation.

In some cases, benefits of environmental policy might come at the cost of the welfare of some communities. Policies promoting adoption of electric vehicles to decarbonise transport can bring environmental benefits for the urban population, but this may reduce the air quality for the population living near power plants in rural areas (Holland et al., 2019[139]). Preventing the disadvantaged groups from bearing the disproportionate burden of policy is critical for ensuring inclusivity, but also for sustaining public support for environmental and climate policy more broadly (Mackie and Haščič, 2019[140]).

Existing empirical evidence suggests that environmental policy will have heterogeneous impacts at different levels of aggregation (OECD, 2021[141]). Consideration of distribution of the costs and benefits of environmental policy is rising in importance, as countries engage in profound social and economic transformation to address environmental challenges. The literature finds inequitable outcomes of environmental policy can arise through: (i) spatial effects, (ii) impact on labour markets and (iii) impact on household income. While there is an expanding body of literature, including studies that capture the dynamic effects of the economic transformation through modelling analysis (e.g. (Borgonovi et al., 2023[142])), it remains an important area that warrants further research to improve the design of environmental policy.

### Spatial effects

Measures seeking to address environmental justice concerns, such as geographically circumscribed regulations, cleaning up the most polluted neighbourhoods or areas, and improve access to amenities (e.g. brownfield development) can improve the environmental quality for the communities facing disproportionate exposure to environmental hazards (Currie, Voorheis and Walker, 2023[143]). However, they can also indirectly bring negative distributional consequences if they are not thoughtfully designed. For instance, improved environmental quality can drive up the market value of houses in the affected areas. Subsequently, environmental improvements may attract higher income households while crowding out certain socio-economic groups, including low-income households and racialised minorities (Melstrom et al., 2022[144]); an unintended consequence documented in many neighbourhoods around the world (Wolch, Byrne and Newell, 2014[145]). This can occur both through demand and supply-side mechanisms, with housing demand from those who are more willing and able to pay more for higher environmental quality increasing the house prices and rents, as well as inelastic housing supply exacerbating the exclusionary dynamics (OECD, 2022[146]).[26]

However, there are important nuances for these spatial effects. The literature typically distinguishes between the impacts on homeowners and renters, with research reaching diverging conclusions. There is evidence demonstrating that the benefits accrue to homeowners in the cleaned-up areas, while resulting in rent increase that can drive those less able to pay to less expensive neighbourhoods (Sieg et al., 2004[147]). Others find that the rents are less responsive to improvements in environmental quality (Grainger, 2012[148]), implying progressive impact of environmental policy.[27] While less recognised, policies that preserve environmental amenities can also bring unintended consequences in in nearby areas. For instance, excessive focus on preserving abundant green space in urban areas can trigger leapfrog development in peri-urban areas, resulting in higher environmental damages (OECD, 2022[146]).

The risk of environmental policy leading to inequitable spatial distribution of benefits (e.g. reduced pollution) also warrants consideration. As instruments such as the emissions trading systems induce firms facing low abatement costs to reduce more emissions, benefits might accrue disproportionately to the communities located near or downwind of these firms (Cain et al., 2023[71]). While much of the existing empirical studies on the impact of market-based policies suggest that this has not been the case to date (Fowlie, Holland and Mansur, 2011[149]; Shapiro and Walker, 2021[10]), there remain ambiguities relating to the spatial distribution of abatement costs and the communities. For instance, some research that consider the non-uniform pollution dispersion finds evidence of disproportionate benefits accruing to high income areas (Grainger and Ruangmas, 2018[150]). Importantly, the risks for uneven distribution of benefits also need to be considered in relation to the aggregate magnitude of environmental improvements across different types of policy instruments (Vona, 2021[151]).

### Labour market implications

Another inequitable distribution of costs could arise from the ramifications of environmental policy for the labour market. The literature suggests that environmental policy induces the substitution from labour to (labour-saving) technology, particularly in the long term (*ibid*). Adoption of cleaner, capital-intensive technologies in response to stringent environmental policy can result in reduced demand for labour and lower wages, disproportionately affecting low-skilled and low-paid workers (Marin and Vona, 2019[152]; Bento, 2013[153]). While empirical evidence suggests the magnitude of this impact is relatively modest, it can compound the uneven distribution of wealth to create further vulnerabilities, as the wages are the main source of income for the poorest and the most disadvantaged.

As the concept of just transition helps illustrate (International Labour Organization, 2016[59]), there are paramount concerns over the disruptive implications of the climate transition for employment opportunities, heightening the sense of unfairness among affected communities. While the transition to more environmentally sustainable economies is a global macroeconomic trend, it will have inherently localised impact, which may be particularly acutely felt in emission-intensive sectors as well as the regions with high concentration of these industries (OECD, 2023[154]). Oft-cited examples are concentrated job losses in coal industry, but they have broader economic implications for hosting communities and the local economy through reduced consumption and weakened local tax base (Carley and Konisky, 2020[155]).

Importantly, environmental policy interacts with broader social and macroeconomic trends such as technological transformation. Changes in the skillsets[28] demanded in the labour market over the course of the green and digital ("twin") transition, as well as existing inequities in educational attainment and access to opportunities for skill development and retraining can give rise to new forms of vulnerabilities (OECD, 2023[156]). These impacts further highlight the need for reskilling and upskilling policies to ensure the transition to a carbon neutral economy does not create or compound new vulnerabilities (Borgonovi et al., 2023[142]).

#### *Impact on household income*

There is a wealth of studies exploring the potential regressivity of environmental policy, highlighting the risks of low-income households bearing disproportionate cost of environmental policy. For instance, higher energy price resulting from environmental policy may affect low income households more, who spend disproportionate portion of their income on energy bills (Bento, 2013[153]).[29] The regressivity impact is further amplified by general tendency of low-income people to live in energy inefficient dwellings and own inefficient appliances across countries (e.g. (Schleich, 2019[157])). While the regressivity of policy varies by the type of fuel and by country, existing evidence underscores the importance of choice of instruments and their design.

Typically, market-based policies instruments are perceived to be more regressive than regulations and standards due to the visibility of their burden (Mackie and Haščič, 2019[140]). However, the evidence suggests that the opposite can be true, particularly as regulations and standards do not generate revenues that can be redistributed to alleviate the burden on low-income households. The burden from market-based instruments such as an energy tax can also vary *within* income groups, compounding the challenge of policy sequencing and design of the alleviating measures (Pizer and Sexton, 2019[158]). For instance, low-income groups in rural areas with insufficient access to public transport may bear greater burdens of taxes on transport fuels than those in urban areas. While distributional implications of regulations remain relatively less explored in the literature, studies on fuel standards (Davis and Knittel, 2019[159]) and building energy codes (Bruegge, Deryugina and Myers, 2019[160]) find some evidence of regressive impacts.

A growing body of empirical literature suggests patterns of uneven distribution of benefits of environmental policies. Subsidies that uniformly lower the cost of investment in low-carbon solutions may disproportionately benefit high-income households. Home investments such as improved insulation and solar panels tend to be made by homeowners and higher-income households, who face lower credit constraints (Ameli and Brandt, 2014[161]). Similarly, electric vehicles subsidies can also have significant distributional effects as higher-income households are more likely to be able to afford them (Borenstein and Davis, 2016[162]). A better understanding of the net impact of incidence of costs and benefits, and how it is distributed across different segments of the population, is critical for informing the better design of environmental policy (Bento, 2013[153]).

### 2.3.3. Barriers to access to information, participation in decision-making and legal recourse

As the evidence documenting inequitable exposure to environmental harms demonstrates, processes (access to participation, information, and legal recourse, and the lack thereof) are central to understanding how the inequitable distributional outcomes are derived. These procedural rights can be considered mutually reinforcing "access rights" that underpin procedural environmental justice (Gellers and Jeffords, 2018[163]).

#### Barriers to access to information

While many governments commit to greater accessibility of information on the state of the environment, some barriers to access appear to persist. Importantly, availability of environmental information does not necessarily translate into the effective use of information. For instance, technical language often used in information on environmental conditions might limit the scope of how the communities can use the information intended to serve the purpose of enhancing their resilience (Mabon, 2020[164]). As recognised in the Escazú Agreement, marginalised communities may experience challenges regarding literacy and linguistic isolation, or lack knowledge on how to formulate requests for information (Barritt, 2020[49]).

With studies finding that the effective use of environmental information depends on socio-economic factors including educational attainment (Shapiro, 2005[165]), simply making more information available without adequate consideration of the barriers to the use of information can inadvertently amplify the adverse outcomes for vulnerable communities. For instance, mandated disclosure of pollution source to empower vulnerable communities can have the unintended impact of incentivising facilities to relocate to low-income areas (Wang et al., 2021[166]). In this context, the OECD Council Recommendation on Environmental Information and Reporting notes the need to "support educational efforts towards enabling the public to make use of available environmental information" (OECD, 2022[167]).

The nature of the information itself, its scale, scope and relevance for the community in question are also key to determining its eventual use. Historically, environmental information made available to the public has often been issue-specific, with countries commonly publishing the data on environmental pollution and the chemical releases documented in an inventory (Haklay, 2003[168]). While data disclosure is essential for facilitating and enabling academic research, vulnerable communities may need more processed and interpreted information; for instance, the primary interest of those who experience asthma is whether they will likely suffer an attack, rather than the level of ground-level air pollution (*ibid*).

#### Barriers to access to participation in decision making

Addressing barriers to participation in environmental decision-making is critical for alleviating inequitable environmental burdens on vulnerable communities (Freudenberg, Pastor and Israel, 2011[169]). Even when the right to participate is legally protected, there remains an inherent flexibility in the modalities and forms participation take in practice (Barritt, 2020[49]). Modalities of participatory processes can also constitute barriers to meaningful participation. Formal policy consultations, while laudable in intent, may not always lend themselves well to consideration of the breadth of views (OECD, 2023[170]). There appears to be a sense of disillusionment in the processes, with over 40% of people in OECD countries stating that governments are unlikely to adopt inputs from public consultations (*ibid*).

Even if opportunities are available and formally open for anyone to participate, some communities, including those less equipped with resources (e.g. language, time, internet connection), can still be excluded from participatory opportunities (Karner et al., 2018[171]). Without adequate recognition of existing barriers and biases, increasing participatory opportunities might reinforce existing inequalities (*ibid*). There is a risk of self-selection bias, with open calls for participants typically attracting participants who are more likely to be older, male, well-educated, affluent and urban (OECD, 2022[172]). Past examples of community engagement suggest that poorly designed participatory processes can even leave communities frustrated and discourage them from further participation (Ruano-Chamorro, Gurney and Cinner, 2022[173]).

While lack of meaningful participation in environmental decision-making is problematic in its own right, it can also stall progress for the transition to more environmentally sustainable economies. For instance, while the public generally supports renewables, this has not always translated into support for the development of renewable energy infrastructure in their communities (Wolsink, 2007[174]), with patterns of public dissatisfaction about the processes of decision-making observed across the world (van de Grift and Cuppen, 2022[175]). While there is no conclusive evidence explaining the seemingly conflicting patterns of broad public support and strong local oppositions (Carley et al., 2020[176]), lack of adequate participation in decision-making is often highlighted as one of the key drivers of opposition (Suškevičs et al., 2019[177]).[30] Mechanistic application of participation as a bureaucratic process and a validation exercise of the decisions that are already made may not adequately substantiate the right to participation (Armeni, 2016[178]; Wesselink et al., 2011[179]). Designing participatory mechanisms that ensure communities can meaningfully affect the outcomes might generate greater support, which in turn can propel the transition (Walker and Baxter, 2017[180]).

### *Barriers to access to legal recourse*

Legal recourse has also been recognised as an important enabling factor for resolution of conflicts and protection of rights for marginalised communities (Scheidel et al., 2020[181]). Although relatively little is understood about the barriers to access to justice in environmental matters, it is often considered the procedural pillar that has historically lagged behind across countries (Mauerhofer, 2016[182]). The wider literature on access to justice also suggests that availability and quality of legal recourse is influenced by social and economic variables (OECD and Open Society Foundations, 2016[183]). In particular, costs of obtaining legal representation can also be prohibitive, adding to opportunity costs (e.g. missed time at work and care-giving responsibilities). Across most countries, people living in poverty face greater barriers to access to justice although they are more likely to be in need of legal assistance (World Justice Project, 2023[184]); a problem often compounded further by the shortage of personnel and resources for public legal assistance (McDonald, 2021[185]). Furthermore, existing studies suggest that many do not consider the issues they face as legal issues or actively seek and identify legal remedies available (OECD, 2019[186]), which may reflect limited legal knowledge as well as broader lack of trust in courts and legal system (OECD, 2022[187]).

## References

Adamkiewicz, G. et al. (2011), "Moving environmental justice indoors: Understanding structural influences on residential exposure patterns in low-income communities", *American Journal of Public Health*, Vol. 101/SUPPL. 1, https://doi.org/10.2105/AJPH.2011.300119. [117]

Agyeman, J., R. Bullard and B. Evans (2002), "Exploring the Nexus: Bringing together sustainability, environmental justice and equity", *Space and Polity*, Vol. 6/1, https://doi.org/10.1080/13562570220137907. [54]

Agyeman, J. et al. (2016), *Trends and Directions in Environmental Justice: From Inequity to Everyday Life, Community, and Just Sustainabilities*, https://doi.org/10.1146/annurev-environ-110615-090052. [52]

Akese, G. and P. Little (2018), "Electronic Waste and the Environmental Justice Challenge in Agbogbloshie", *Environmental Justice*, Vol. 11/2, https://doi.org/10.1089/env.2017.0039. [40]

Aldinger, P. (2013), "Addressing environmental justice concerns in developing countries: Mining in Nigeria, Uganda and Ghana", *Geo. Int'l Envtl. L. Rev.*, Vol. 26. [37]

Allaire, M. and S. Acquah (2022), "Disparities in drinking water compliance: Implications for incorporating equity into regulatory practices", *AWWA Water Science*, Vol. 4/2, https://doi.org/10.1002/aws2.1274. [99]

Ameli, N. and N. Brandt (2014), "Determinants of Households' Investment in Energy Efficiency and Renewables: Evidence from the OECD Survey on Household Environmental Behaviour and Attitudes", *OECD Economics Department Working Papers*, No. 1165, OECD Publishing, Paris, https://doi.org/10.1787/5jxwtlchggzn-en. [161]

Andrade-Goffe, D., C. Excell and A. Sanhueza (2023), *The Escazú Agreement: Seeking Rights to Information, Participation, and Justice for the Most Vulnerable in Latin America and the Caribbean*, https://www.wri.org/research/escazu-agreement-seeking-rights-information-participation-and-justice-most-vulnerable#:~:text=The%20Escaz%C3%BA%20Agreement%20is%20the,and%20environmental%20human%20rights%20defenders. [51]

Armeni, C. (2016), "Participation in environmental decision-making: Reflecting on planning and community benefits for major wind farms", *Journal of Environmental Law*, Vol. 28/3, https://doi.org/10.1093/jel/eqw021. [178]

Australian Institute of Aboriginal and Torres Strait Isander Studies (n.d.), *Welcome to Country*, https://aiatsis.gov.au/explore/welcome-country (accessed on 23 April 2024). [194]

Banza, C. et al. (2009), "High human exposure to cobalt and other metals in Katanga, a mining area of the Democratic Republic of Congo", *Environmental Research*, Vol. 109/6, https://doi.org/10.1016/j.envres.2009.04.012. [38]

Banzhaf, H., L. Ma and C. Timmins (2019), *Environmental Justice: Establishing Causal Relationships*, https://doi.org/10.1146/annurev-resource-100518-094131. [9]

Banzhaf, S., L. Ma and C. Timmins (2019), "Environmental justice: The economics of race, place, and pollution", *Journal of Economic Perspectives*, Vol. 33/1, https://doi.org/10.1257/jep.33.1.185. [70]

Barnes, J., T. Chatterton and J. Longhurst (2019), "Emissions vs exposure: Increasing injustice from road traffic-related air pollution in the United Kingdom", *Transportation Research Part D: Transport and Environment*, Vol. 73, https://doi.org/10.1016/j.trd.2019.05.012. [132]

Barritt, E. (2020), "Global values, transnational expression: from Aarhus to Escazú", in *Research Handbook on Transnational Environmental Law*, https://doi.org/10.4337/9781788119634.00022. [49]

Been, V. (1994), "Locally Undesirable Land Uses in Minority Neighborhoods: Disproportionate Siting or Market Dynamics?", *Yale Law Journal*, Vol. 103/6, pp. 1383-1422, https://www.jstor.org/stable/797089. [65]

Bell, D. and J. Carrick (2017), "Procedural environmental justice", in *The Routledge Handbook of Environmental Justice*. [19]

Bell, K. (2014), *Achieving environmental justice: A cross-national analysis.* [33]

Bento, A. (2013), *Equity impacts of environmental policy*, https://doi.org/10.1146/annurev-resource-091912-151925. [153]

Bento, A., M. Freedman and C. Lang (2015), "Who benefits from environmental regulation? Evidence from the clean air act amendments", *Review of Economics and Statistics*, Vol. 97/3, https://doi.org/10.1162/REST_a_00493. [193]

Borenstein, S. and L. Davis (2016), "The distributional effects of US clean energy tax credits", *Tax Policy and the Economy*, Vol. 30/1, https://doi.org/10.1086/685597. [162]

Borgonovi, F. et al. (2023), "The effects of the EU Fit for 55 package on labour markets and the demand for skills", *OECD Social, Employment and Migration Working Papers*. [142]

Boyd, D. (2023), *Statement at the conclusion of country visit to Chile*, https://www.ohchr.org/sites/default/files/documents/issues/environment/srenvironment/eom-statement-Chile-12-May-2023-EN.pdf. [96]

Boyles, A. et al. (2021), "Environmental Factors Involved in Maternal Morbidity and Mortality", *Journal of Women's Health*, Vol. 30/2, https://doi.org/10.1089/jwh.2020.8855. [127]

Brown, P. (1997), "Popular Epidemiology Revisited", *Current Sociology*, Vol. 45/3, https://doi.org/10.1177/001139297045003008. [122]

Bruckner, B. et al. (2022), "Impacts of poverty alleviation on national and global carbon emissions", *Nature Sustainability*, Vol. 5/4, https://doi.org/10.1038/s41893-021-00842-z. [53]

Bruegge, C., T. Deryugina and E. Myers (2019), "The distributional effects of building energy codes", *Journal of the Association of Environmental and Resource Economists*, Vol. 6/S1, https://doi.org/10.1086/701189. [160]

Brulle, R. and D. Pellow (2006), *Environmental justice: Human health and environmental inequalities*, https://doi.org/10.1146/annurev.publhealth.27.021405.102124. [123]

Bullard, R. (1990), *Dumping in Dixie: Race, class, and environmental quality*, Boulder, Colo: Westview Press. [66]

Bullard, R. (1983), "Solid Waste Sites and the Black Houston Community", *Sociological Inquiry*, Vol. 53/2-3, https://doi.org/10.1111/j.1475-682X.1983.tb00037.x. [8]

Bullard, R. and B. Wright (2018), "Race, place, and the environment in post-Katrina New Orleans", in *Race, Place, and Environmental Justice after Hurricane Katrina: Struggles to Reclaim, Rebuild, and Revitalize New Orleans and the Gulf Coast*, https://doi.org/10.4324/9780429497858. [90]

Burger, J. and M. Gochfeld (2011), "Conceptual environmental justice model for evaluating chemical pathways of exposure in low-income, minority, Native American, and other unique exposure populations", *American Journal of Public Health*, Vol. 101/SUPPL. 1, https://doi.org/10.2105/AJPH.2010.300077. [111]

Cain, L. et al. (2023), "Recent Findings and Methodologies in Economics Research in Environmental Justice", *SSRN Electronic Journal*, https://doi.org/10.2139/ssrn.4368212. [71]

Carley, S. and D. Konisky (2020), *The justice and equity implications of the clean energy transition*, https://doi.org/10.1038/s41560-020-0641-6. [155]

Carley, S. et al. (2020), *Energy infrastructure, NIMBYism, and public opinion: A systematic literature review of three decades of empirical survey literature*, https://doi.org/10.1088/1748-9326/ab875d. [176]

Carruthers, D. (2008), *Environmental justice in Latin America: Problems, promise, and practice*, Mit Press, Cambridge, Massachusetts. [25]

Casey, J. et al. (2024), "Measuring long-term exposure to wildfire PM2.5 in California: Time-varying inequities in environmental burden", *PNAS*, Vol. 121/8, https://doi.org/10.1073/pnas.2306729121. [91]

Chan, H. and O. Receveur (2000), *Mercury in the traditional diet of indigenous peoples in Canada*, https://doi.org/10.1016/S0269-7491(00)00061-0. [112]

Charles, A. and H. Thomas (2007), "Deafness and disability - Forgotten components of environmental justice: Illustrated by the case of Local Agenda 21 in South Wales", *Local Environment*, Vol. 12/3, https://doi.org/10.1080/13549830601183677. [192]

Cock, J. (2006), "Connecting the Red, Brown and Green: The Environmental Justice Movement in South Africa", *Voices of Protest: Social Movements in Post-Apartheid South Africa*. [41]

Collins, H. et al. (2023), "Differences in personal care product use by race/ethnicity among women in California: implications for chemical exposures", *Journal of Exposure Science and Environmental Epidemiology*, Vol. 33/2, https://doi.org/10.1038/s41370-021-00404-7. [116]

Collins, M., I. Munoz and J. Jaja (2016), "Linking 'toxic outliers' to environmental justice communities", *Environmental Research Letters*, Vol. 11/1, https://doi.org/10.1088/1748-9326/11/1/015004. [102]

Collins, T. and S. Grineski (2018), "Environmental justice and flood hazards", in *The Routledge Handbook of Environmental Justice*, https://doi.org/10.4324/9781315678986-28. [89]

Colmer, J. et al. (2020), "Disparities in PM2.5 air pollution in the United States", *Science*, Vol. 369/6503, https://doi.org/10.1126/science.aaz9353. [138]

Currie, J. (2011), *Inequality at birth: Some causes and consequences*, https://doi.org/10.1257/aer.101.3.1. [135]

Currie, J., J. Voorheis and R. Walker (2023), "What Caused Racial Disparities in Particulate Exposure to Fall? New Evidence from the Clean Air Act and Satellite-Based Measures of Air Quality", *American Economic Review*, Vol. 113/1, https://doi.org/10.1257/aer.20191957. [143]

Dai, D. (2011), "Racial/ethnic and socioeconomic disparities in urban green space accessibility: Where to intervene?", *Landscape and Urban Planning*, Vol. 102/4, https://doi.org/10.1016/j.landurbplan.2011.05.002. [107]

Davis, L. and C. Knittel (2019), "Are fuel economy standards regressive?", *Journal of the Association of Environmental and Resource Economists*, Vol. 6/S1, https://doi.org/10.1086/701187. [159]

Debbané, A. and R. Keil (2004), "Multiple disconnections: Environmental justice and urban water in Canada and South Africa", *Space and Polity*, Vol. 8/2, https://doi.org/10.1080/1356257042000273968. [2]

Deb, N. (2023), *Unyielding humanity from catastrophic ruins:new political society for social and environmental justice after Bhopal*. [86]

Dillman, K. and J. Heinonen (2022), "A 'just' hydrogen economy: A normative energy justice assessment of the hydrogen economy", *Renewable and Sustainable Energy Reviews*, Vol. 167, https://doi.org/10.1016/j.rser.2022.112648. [78]

Doremus, J., I. Jacqz and S. Johnston (2022), "Sweating the energy bill: Extreme weather, poor households, and the energy spending gap", *Journal of Environmental Economics and Management*, Vol. 112, https://doi.org/10.1016/j.jeem.2022.102609. [97]

Eckerman, I. and T. Børsen (2021), "Corporate and governmental responsibilities for preventing chemical disasters: Lessons from Bhopal", in *Ethics Of Chemistry: From Poison Gas To Climate Engineering*, https://doi.org/10.1142/9789811233548_0005. [85]

Economic Commission for Latin America and the Caribbean (2022), *Background*, https://acuerdodeescazu.cepal.org/cop1/en/background (accessed on 23 April 2024). [28]

Economic Commission for Latin America and the Caribbean (2018), *Regional Agreement on Access to Information, Public Participation and Justice in Environmental Matters in Latin America and the Caribbean*, https://repositorio.cepal.org/items/86cae662-f81c-4b45-a04a-058e8d26143c (accessed on 23 April 2024). [48]

European Commission (2021), *Guidance note on the collection and the use of equality data based on racial or ethnic origin*, https://doi.org/10.2838/06180. [200]

European Commission (n.d.), *Single Entry Point*, https://trade.ec.europa.eu/access-to-markets/en/content/single-entry-point-0 (accessed on 23 April 2024). [81]

European Commission (n.d.), *The Aarhus Convention and the EU*, https://environment.ec.europa.eu/law-and-governance/aarhus_en (accessed on 23 April 2024). [47]

European Environment Agency (2018), *Unequal exposure and unequal impacts: social vulnerability to air pollution, noise and extreme temperatures in Europe*, https://www.eea.europa.eu/publications/unequal-exposure-and-unequal-impacts/ (accessed on 23 April 2024). [22]

Ezell, J. et al. (2021), *The blueprint of disaster: COVID-19, the Flint water crisis, and unequal ecological impacts*, https://doi.org/10.1016/S2542-5196(21)00076-0. [95]

Fairburn, J., W. Maier and M. Braubach (2016), *Incorporating environmental justice into second generation indices of multiple deprivation: Lessons from the UK and progress internationally*, https://doi.org/10.3390/ijerph13080750. [21]

Fan, M. and K. Chou (2017), "Environmental justice in a transitional and transboundary context in east Asia", in *The Routledge Handbook of Environmental Justice*, https://doi.org/10.4324/9781315678986-49. [30]

Finewood, M. et al. (2023), "The Bronx River and Environmental Justice Through the Lens of a Watershed", *Case Studies in the Environment*, Vol. 7/1, https://doi.org/10.1525/cse.2023.1824941. [73]

Foerster, A. (2019), "Climate Justice and Corporations", *King's Law Journal*, Vol. 30/2, https://doi.org/10.1080/09615768.2019.1645447. [83]

Fossa, A. et al. (2023), "Sociodemographic correlates of greenness within public parks in three U.S. cities", *Wellbeing, Space and Society*, Vol. 5, https://doi.org/10.1016/j.wss.2023.100157. [108]

Fowlie, M., S. Holland and E. Mansur (2011), "What Do Emissions Markets Deliver and to Whom? Evidence from Southern California's NOx Trading Program", *SSRN Electronic Journal*, https://doi.org/10.2139/ssrn.1416787. [149]

Franchini, M. and P. Mannucci (2018), *Mitigation of air pollution by greenness: A narrative review*, https://doi.org/10.1016/j.ejim.2018.06.021. [105]

Fraser, N. (2000), *Rethinking recognition*. [45]

Freudenberg, N., M. Pastor and B. Israel (2011), "Strengthening community capacity to participate in making decisions to reduce disproportionate environmental exposures", *American Journal of Public Health*, Vol. 101/SUPPL. 1, https://doi.org/10.2105/AJPH.2011.300265. [169]

Gallagher, K. (ed.) (2008), *The global waste trade and environmental justice struggles*, Edward Elgar Publishing, Inc. [76]

Garsous, G. and S. Worack (2021), "Trade as a channel for environmental technologies diffusion: The case of the wind turbine manufacturing industry", *Oecd*. [80]

Gellers, J. and C. Jeffords (2018), "Toward environmental democracy? Procedural environmental rights and environmental justice", *Global Environmental Politics*, Vol. 18/1, https://doi.org/10.1162/GLEP_a_00445. [163]

Gibbons, E. (2014), "Climate change, children's rights, and the pursuit of intergenerational climate justice", *Health and Human Rights*, Vol. 16/1. [57]

Global Environmental Justice Atlas (2024), *EJAtlas - Global Atlas of Environmental Justice*, https://ejatlas.org/ (accessed on 23 April 2024). [42]

Global Witness (2022), *Decade of defiance*, https://www.globalwitness.org/en/campaigns/environmental-activists/decade-defiance/#a-global-analysis-2021 (accessed on 23 April 2024). [204]

Grainger, C. (2012), "The distributional effects of pollution regulations: Do renters fully pay for cleaner air?", *Journal of Public Economics*, Vol. 96/9-10, https://doi.org/10.1016/j.jpubeco.2012.06.006. [148]

Grainger, C. and T. Ruangmas (2018), "Who Wins from Emissions Trading? Evidence from California", *Environmental and Resource Economics*, Vol. 71/3, https://doi.org/10.1007/s10640-017-0180-1. [150]

Hacon, S. et al. (2020), "Mercury exposure through fish consumption in traditional communities in the Brazilian Northern Amazon", *International Journal of Environmental Research and Public Health*, Vol. 17/15, https://doi.org/10.3390/ijerph17155269. [113]

Hajat, A., C. Hsia and M. O'Neill (2015), *Socioeconomic Disparities and Air Pollution Exposure: a Global Review*, https://doi.org/10.1007/s40572-015-0069-5. [63]

Haklay, M. (2003), "Public access to environmental information: Past, present and future", *Computers, Environment and Urban Systems*, Vol. 27/2, https://doi.org/10.1016/S0198-9715(01)00023-0. [168]

Haklay, M. and L. Francis (2017), "Participatory GIS and community-based citizen science for environmental justice action", in *The Routledge Handbook of Environmental Justice*, https://doi.org/10.4324/9781315678986-24. [191]

Hallegatte, S. et al. (2020), "From Poverty to Disaster and Back: a Review of the Literature", *Economics of Disasters and Climate Change*, Vol. 4/1, https://doi.org/10.1007/s41885-020-00060-5. [61]

Hall, J. and P. Lukey (2023), "Public participation as an essential requirement of the environmental rule of law: Reflections on South Africa's approach in policy and practice", *African Human Rights Law Journal*, pp. 303-332, https://doi.org/10.17159/1996-2096/2023/v23n2a4. [36]

Heidegger, P. and K. Wiese (2020), *Pushed to the wastelands: environmental racism against Roma communities in Central and Eastern Europe*, https://eeb.org/wp-content/uploads/2020/04/Pushed-to-the-Wastelands.pdf. [23]

Holland, S. et al. (2019), "Distributional effects of air pollution from electric vehicle adoption", *Journal of the Association of Environmental and Resource Economists*, Vol. 6/S1, https://doi.org/10.1086/701188. [139]

Hopkins, E. et al. (2023), "Can the equitable roll out of electric vehicle charging infrastructure be achieved?", *Renewable and Sustainable Energy Reviews*, Vol. 182, https://doi.org/10.1016/j.rser.2023.113398. [110]

Hu, H. and G. Huang (2014), "Monitoring of non-point source pollutions from an agriculture watershed in South China", *Water (Switzerland)*, Vol. 6/12, https://doi.org/10.3390/w6123828. [190]

Hyland, C. and O. Laribi (2017), *Review of take-home pesticide exposure pathway in children living in agricultural areas*, https://doi.org/10.1016/j.envres.2017.04.017. [120]

Intergovernmental Panel on Climate Change (2023), "IPCC, 2022: Annex II: Glossary", in *Climate Change 2022 – Impacts, Adaptation and Vulnerability. Contribution of Working Group II to the Sixth Assessment Report of the Intergovernmental Panel on Climate Change*. [58]

International Labour Organization (2016), *Guidelines for a just transition towards environmentally sustainable economies and societies for all*, https://www.ilo.org/global/topics/green-jobs/publications/WCMS_432859/lang--en/index.htm (accessed on 23 April 2024). [59]

James, P. et al. (2015), "A Review of the Health Benefits of Greenness", *Current Epidemiology Reports*, Vol. 2/2, https://doi.org/10.1007/s40471-015-0043-7. [104]

Jenkins, K. (2018), *Setting energy justice apart from the crowd: Lessons from environmental and climate justice*, https://doi.org/10.1016/j.erss.2017.11.015. [62]

Johnston, J. and L. Cushing (2020), *Chemical Exposures, Health, and Environmental Justice in Communities Living on the Fenceline of Industry*, https://doi.org/10.1007/s40572-020-00263-8. [93]

Karasaki, S. et al. (2023), *Environmental justice and drinking water: A critical review of primary data studies*, https://doi.org/10.1002/wat2.1653. [75]

Karner, A. et al. (2018), "Transportation and environmental justice", in *The Routledge Handbook of Environmental Justice*, https://doi.org/10.4324/9781315678986-32. [171]

Klemick, H. et al. (2024), "Factors Influencing Customer Participation in a Program to Replace Lead Pipes for Drinking Water", *Environmental and Resource Economics*, Vol. 87, pp. 791-832, https://doi.org/10.1007/s10640-023-00836-9. [98]

Knoble, C. and D. Yu (2023), *Environmental justice: An evolving concept in a dynamic era*, https://doi.org/10.1002/sd.2519. [100]

Köckler, H. et al. (2017), "Environmental justice in western Europe", in *The Routledge Handbook of Environmental Justice*, https://doi.org/10.4324/9781315678986-50. [20]

Kravchenko, J. et al. (2018), "Mortality and Health Outcomes in North Carolina Communities Located in Close Proximity to Hog Concentrated Animal Feeding Operations", *North Carolina medical journal*, Vol. 79/5, https://doi.org/10.18043/ncm.79.5.278. [69]

Landrigan, P., V. Rauh and M. Galvez (2010), "Environmental justice and the health of children", *Mount Sinai Journal of Medicine*, Vol. 77/2, https://doi.org/10.1002/msj.20173. [129]

Lee, S. et al. (2015), "Relationship between non-point source pollution and Korean green factor", *Terrestrial, Atmospheric and Oceanic Sciences*, Vol. 26/3, https://doi.org/10.3319/TAO.2014.11.10.01(Hy). [189]

Mabon, L. (2020), "Making climate information services accessible to communities: What can we learn from environmental risk communication research?", *Urban Climate*, Vol. 31, https://doi.org/10.1016/j.uclim.2019.100537. [164]

Mackie, A. and I. Haščič (2019), "The distributional aspects of environmental quality and environmental policies: Opportunities for individuals and households", *OECD Green Growth Papers*, No. 2019/02, OECD Publishing, Paris, https://doi.org/10.1787/e0939b52-en. [140]

Manisalidis, I. et al. (2020), *Environmental and Health Impacts of Air Pollution: A Review*, https://doi.org/10.3389/fpubh.2020.00014. [64]

Mannan, M. and S. Al-Ghamdi (2021), *Indoor air quality in buildings: A comprehensive review on the factors influencing air pollution in residential and commercial structure*, https://doi.org/10.3390/ijerph18063276. [118]

Marin, G. and F. Vona (2019), "Climate policies and skill-biased employment dynamics: Evidence from EU countries", *Journal of Environmental Economics and Management*, Vol. 98, https://doi.org/10.1016/j.jeem.2019.102253. [152]

Marlow, T., J. Elliott and S. Frickel (2022), "Future flooding increases unequal exposure risks to relic industrial pollution", *Environmental Research Letters*, Vol. 17/7, https://doi.org/10.1088/1748-9326/ac78f7. [94]

Martínez Alier, J. (2020), "A global environmental justice movement: mapping ecological distribution conflicts", *Disjuntiva. Crítica de les Ciències Socials*, Vol. 1/2, https://doi.org/10.14198/disjuntiva2020.1.2.6. [84]

Martinez-Alier, J. (2001), "Mining conflicts, environmental justice, and valuation", *Journal of Hazardous Materials*, Vol. 86/1-3, https://doi.org/10.1016/S0304-3894(01)00252-7. [39]

Martinez-Alier, J. et al. (2016), "Is there a global environmental justice movement?", *Journal of Peasant Studies*, Vol. 43/3, https://doi.org/10.1080/03066150.2016.1141198. [5]

Mauerhofer, V. (2016), "Public participation in environmental matters: Compendium, challenges and chances globally", *Land Use Policy*, Vol. 52, https://doi.org/10.1016/j.landusepol.2014.12.012. [182]

McCauley, D. and R. Heffron (2018), "Just transition: Integrating climate, energy and environmental justice", *Energy Policy*, Vol. 119, https://doi.org/10.1016/j.enpol.2018.04.014. [60]

McCord, G. et al. (2023), "Long-term health and human capital effects of in utero exposure to an industrial disaster: A spatial difference-in-differences analysis of the Bhopal gas tragedy", *BMJ Open*, Vol. 13/6, https://doi.org/10.1136/bmjopen-2022-066733. [87]

McDonald, D. (ed.) (2002), *What is environmental justice?*, Ohio University Press. [34]

McDonald, D. (ed.) (2002), *Workplace environmental justice: trade unions and the struggle for an ecological platform.*, Ohio University Press. [35]

McDonald, H. (2021), "Assessing Access to Justice: How Much "Legal" Do People Need and How Can We Know?", *UC Irvine Law Review*, Vol. 11/3, https://scholarship.law.uci.edu/ucilr/vol11/iss3/6. [185]

Melstrom, R. et al. (2022), "Who Benefits From Brownfield Cleanup and Gentrification? Evidence From Chicago", *Urban Affairs Review*, Vol. 58/6, https://doi.org/10.1177/10780874211041537. [144]

Ministry for the Environment (2022), *Māori Climate Platform*, https://environment.govt.nz/what-government-is-doing/areas-of-work/climate-change/maori-climate-platform/. [32]

Mitchell, G. (2019), "The messy challenge of environmental justice in the UK: evolution, status and prospects", *Natural England Commissioned Report NECR273*, https://eprints.whiterose.ac.uk/148740/1/2019%20Mitchell%20NE%20EJ%20commissioned%20report%20NECR273.pdf. [18]

Mohai, P., D. Pellow and J. Roberts (2009), "Environmental justice", *Annual Review of Environment and Resources*, Vol. 34, https://doi.org/10.1146/annurev-environ-082508-094348. [14]

Mohai, P. and R. Saha (2015), "Which came first, people or pollution? Assessing the disparate siting and post-siting demographic change hypotheses of environmental injustice", *Environmental Research Letters*, Vol. 10/11, https://doi.org/10.1088/1748-9326/10/11/115008. [101]

Morello-Frosch, R. and E. Shenassa (2006), *The environmental "Riskscape" and social inequality: Implications for explaining maternal and child health disparities*, https://doi.org/10.1289/ehp.8930. [128]

Müller, F., J. Tunn and T. Kalt (2022), "Hydrogen justice", *Environmental Research Letters*, Vol. 17/11, https://doi.org/10.1088/1748-9326/ac991a. [77]

OECD (2024), *Mainstreaming Biodiversity into Renewable Power Infrastructure*, OECD Publishing, Paris, https://doi.org/10.1787/357ac474-en. [198]

OECD (2023), *Government at a Glance 2023*, OECD Publishing, Paris, https://doi.org/10.1787/3d5c5d31-en. [170]

OECD (2023), *Job Creation and Local Economic Development 2023: Bridging the Great Green Divide*, OECD Publishing, Paris, https://doi.org/10.1787/21db61c1-en. [154]

OECD (2023), *OECD Environmental Performance Reviews: United States 2023*, OECD Environmental Performance Reviews, OECD Publishing, Paris, https://doi.org/10.1787/47675117-en. [11]

OECD (2023), *OECD Skills Outlook 2023: Skills for a Resilient Green and Digital Transition*, OECD Publishing, Paris, https://doi.org/10.1787/27452f29-en. [156]

OECD (2023), *OECD work on Regional Trade Agreements and the environment. Policy Perspectives*, https://www2.oecd.org/env/Policy-Perspectives-OECD-work-on-regional-trade-agreements-and-the-environment.pdf. [82]

OECD (2022), *Building Trust to Reinforce Democracy: Main Findings from the 2021 OECD Survey on Drivers of Trust in Public Institutions*, Building Trust in Public Institutions, OECD Publishing, Paris, https://doi.org/10.1787/b407f99c-en. [187]

OECD (2022), *OECD Guidelines for Citizen Participation Processes*, OECD Public Governance Reviews, OECD Publishing, Paris, https://doi.org/10.1787/22190414. [172]

OECD (2022), "Provision of urban environmental amenities: A policy toolkit for inclusiveness", *OECD Environment Working Papers*, https://doi.org/10.1787/0866d566-en. [146]

OECD (2022), *Recommendation of the Council on Environmental Information and Reporting*, https://legalinstruments.oecd.org/en/instruments/OECD-LEGAL-0471 (accessed on 23 April 2024). [167]

OECD (2021), *Assessing the Economic Impacts of Environmental Policies: Evidence from a Decade of OECD Research*, OECD Publishing, Paris, https://doi.org/10.1787/bf2fb156-en. [141]

OECD (2019), *Equal Access to Justice for Inclusive Growth: Putting People at the Centre*, OECD Publishing, Paris, https://doi.org/10.1787/597f5b7f-en. [186]

OECD (2019), *Health for Everyone?: Social Inequalities in Health and Health Systems*, OECD Health Policy Studies, OECD Publishing, Paris, https://doi.org/10.1787/3c8385d0-en. [199]

OECD (2018), *OECD Due Diligence Guidance for Responsible Business Conduct*, OECD Publishing, Paris, https://mneguidelines.oecd.org/OECD-Due-Diligence-Guidance-for-Responsible-Business-Conduct.pdf. [88]

OECD (2012), *Water Quality and Agriculture: Meeting the Policy Challenge*, OECD Studies on Water, OECD Publishing, Paris, https://doi.org/10.1787/9789264168060-en. [74]

OECD and Open Society Foundations (2016), *Leveraging the SDGs for Inclusive Growth: Delivering Access to Justice for All*, https://www.oecd.org/gov/delivering-access-to-justice-for-all.pdf. [183]

OHCHR (2018), *A human rights-based approach to data: leaving no one behind in the 2030 agenda for sustainable development*, https://www.ohchr.org/sites/default/files/Documents/Issues/HRIndicators/GuidanceNoteonApproachtoData.pdf. [205]

Park, Y. and M. Kwan (2020), "Understanding racial disparities in exposure to traffic-related air pollution: Considering the spatiotemporal dynamics of population distribution", *International Journal of Environmental Research and Public Health*, Vol. 17/3, https://doi.org/10.3390/ijerph17030908. [133]

Parliament of Canada (2023), *An Act respecting the development of a national strategy to assess, prevent and address environmental racism and to advance environmental justice*, https://www.parl.ca/legisinfo/en/bill/44-1/c-226 (accessed on 23 April 2024). [17]

Philibert, A., M. Fillion and D. Mergler (2020), "Mercury exposure and premature mortality in the Grassy Narrows First Nation community: a retrospective longitudinal study", *The Lancet Planetary Health*, Vol. 4/4, https://doi.org/10.1016/S2542-5196(20)30057-7. [16]

Pizer, W. and S. Sexton (2019), *The Distributional Impacts of Energy Taxes*, https://doi.org/10.1093/reep/rey021. [158]

Prüss-Ustün, A. et al. (2019), "Environmental risks and non-communicable diseases", *BMJ (Online)*, Vol. 364, https://doi.org/10.1136/bmj.l265. [126]

Rasmussen, M. and P. Pinho (2016), "Introduction: Environmental Justice and Climate Change in Latin America", *LASAForum*, Vol. 47/4, https://forum.lasaweb.org/files/vol47-issue4/Debates1.pdf. [24]

Resnik, D. (2022), "Environmental justice and climate change policies", *Bioethics*, Vol. 36/7, https://doi.org/10.1111/bioe.13042. [56]

Ruano-Chamorro, C., G. Gurney and J. Cinner (2022), *Advancing procedural justice in conservation*, https://doi.org/10.1111/conl.12861. [173]

Ruiz, D. et al. (2018), "Disparities in environmental exposures to endocrine-disrupting chemicals and diabetes risk in vulnerable populations", *Diabetes Care*, Vol. 41/1, https://doi.org/10.2337/dc16-2765. [114]

San Sebastián, M. and A. Hurtig (2005), "Oil development and health in the Amazon basin of Ecuador: The popular epidemiology process", *Social Science and Medicine*, Vol. 60/4, https://doi.org/10.1016/j.socscimed.2004.06.016. [124]

Scheidel, A. et al. (2020), "Environmental conflicts and defenders: A global overview", *Global Environmental Change*, Vol. 63, https://doi.org/10.1016/j.gloenvcha.2020.102104. [181]

Schleich, J. (2019), "Energy efficient technology adoption in low-income households in the European Union – What is the evidence?", *Energy Policy*, Vol. 125, https://doi.org/10.1016/j.enpol.2018.10.061. [157]

Schlosberg, D. (2013), "Theorising environmental justice: The expanding sphere of a discourse", *Environmental Politics*, Vol. 22/1, https://doi.org/10.1080/09644016.2013.755387. [4]

Schlosberg, D. (2007), *Defining Environmental Justice: Theories, Movements, and Nature*, https://doi.org/10.1093/acprof:oso/9780199286294.001.0001. [3]

Schlosberg, D. (2004), "Reconceiving environmental justice: Global movements and political theories", *Environmental Politics*, Vol. 13/3, https://doi.org/10.1080/0964401042000229025. [43]

Schlosberg, D. and L. Collins (2014), *From environmental to climate justice: Climate change and the discourse of environmental justice*, https://doi.org/10.1002/wcc.275. [6]

Schlosberg, D., L. Rickards and J. Byrne (2018), "Environmental justice and attachment to place", in *The Routledge Handbook of Environmental Justice*, https://doi.org/10.4324/9781315678986-47. [31]

Shapiro, J. and R. Walker (2021), "Where Is Pollution Moving? Environmental Markets and Environmental Justice", *AEA Papers and Proceedings*, Vol. 111, https://doi.org/10.1257/pandp.20211004. [10]

Shapiro, M. (2005), "Equity and information: Information regulation, environmental justice, and risks from toxic chemicals", *Journal of Policy Analysis and Management*, Vol. 24/2, https://doi.org/10.1002/pam.20094. [165]

Sieg, H. et al. (2004), "Estimating the general equilibrium benefits of large changes in spatially delineated public goods", *International Economic Review*, Vol. 45/4, https://doi.org/10.1111/j.0020-6598.2004.00297.x. [147]

Siroux, V., L. Agier and R. Slama (2016), "The exposome concept: A challenge and a potential driver for environmental health research", *European Respiratory Review*, Vol. 25/140, https://doi.org/10.1183/16000617.0034-2016. [136]

Solomon, G. et al. (2016), *Cumulative Environmental Impacts: Science and Policy to Protect Communities*, https://doi.org/10.1146/annurev-publhealth-032315-021807. [131]

Stein, P. and M. Stein (2022), *Climate change and the right to health of people with disabilities*, https://doi.org/10.1016/S2214-109X(21)00542-8. [92]

Suškevičs, M. et al. (2019), "Regional variation in public acceptance of wind energy development in Europe: What are the roles of planning procedures and participation?", *Land Use Policy*, Vol. 81, https://doi.org/10.1016/j.landusepol.2018.10.032. [177]

Sze, J. and J. London (2008), "Environmental Justice at the Crossroads", *Sociology Compass*, Vol. 2/4, https://doi.org/10.1111/j.1751-9020.2008.00131.x. [67]

Thornhill, I. et al. (2022), "Blue-space availability, environmental quality and amenity use across contrasting socioeconomic contexts", *Applied Geography*, Vol. 144, https://doi.org/10.1016/j.apgeog.2022.102716. [109]

Ulloa, A. (2017), *Perspectives of Environmental Justice from Indigenous Peoples of Latin America: A Relational Indigenous Environmental Justice*, https://doi.org/10.1089/env.2017.0017. [27]

UNECE (1998), *Convention on Access to Information, Public Participation in Decision-Making and Access to Justice in Environmental Matters,*, United Nations, Treaty Series , vol. 2161, https://treaties.un.org/doc/Treaties/1998/06/19980625%2008-35%20AM/Ch_XXVII_13p.pdf. [46]

UNFCCC (2015), *Paris Agreement*, https://unfccc.int/files/meetings/paris_nov_2015/application/pdf/paris_agreement_english_.pdf. [197]

United Nations (2024), *Third meeting of the Conference of the Parties to the Escazú Agreement*, https://acuerdodeescazu.cepal.org/cop3/en/news/cop-3-escazu-agreement-reinforces-commitment-recognize-protect-and-promote-all-rights-human (accessed on 13 May 2024). [29]

United Nations (1992), *Rio Declaration on Environment and Development*, https://www.un.org/en/development/desa/population/migration/generalassembly/docs/globalcompact/A_CONF.151_26_Vol.I_Declaration.pdf. [50]

United Nations Environment Programme (2021), *NEGLECTED: Environmental Justice Impacts of Marine Litter and Plastic Pollution*, https://www.unep.org/resources/report/neglected-environmental-justice-impacts-marine-litter-and-plastic-pollution (accessed on 23 April 2024). [119]

United States Environmental Protection Agency (2023), *Environmental Justice*, https://www.epa.gov/environmentaljustice (accessed on 23 April 2024). [203]

United States Environmental Protection Agency (2023), *EPA Draft Revision of Technical Guidance for Assessing Environmental Justice in Regulatory Analysis*, https://www.epa.gov/system/files/documents/2023-11/ejtg_revision_110823_508compliant_0.pdf. [121]

United States Environmental Protection Agency (2023), *Federal Actions to Address Environmental Justice in Minority Populations and Low-Income Populations*, https://www.epa.gov/environmentaljustice/federal-actions-address-environmental-justice-minority-populations-and-low (accessed on 23 April 2024). [7]

United States Environmental Protection Agency (2023), *Human Exposure and Health*, https://www.epa.gov/report-environment/human-exposure-and-health (accessed on 23 April 2024). [130]

United States Environmental Protection Agency (2022), *EPA Researchers Release Cumulative Impacts Report, Prioritizing Environmental Justice in New Research Cycle*, https://www.epa.gov/sciencematters/epa-researchers-release-cumulative-impacts-report-prioritizing-environmental-justice (accessed on 23 April 2024). [202]

United States General Accounting Office (1982), *Siting of Hazardous Waste Landfills and Their Correlation with Racial and Economic Status of Surrounding Communities*, http://archive.gao.gov/d48t13/121648.pdf. [196]

van de Grift, E. and E. Cuppen (2022), "Beyond the public in controversies: A systematic review on social opposition and renewable energy actors", *Energy Research & Social Science*, Vol. 91, https://doi.org/10.1016/j.erss.2022.102749. [175]

Vásquez, A. et al. (2018), "Urban environmental (in)justice in latin america", in *The Routledge Handbook of Environmental Justice*, https://doi.org/10.4324/9781315678986-44. [26]

Viel, J. et al. (2011), "Environmental justice in a French industrial region: Are polluting industrial facilities equally distributed?", *Health and Place*, Vol. 17/1, https://doi.org/10.1016/j.healthplace.2010.10.007. [68]

Vona, F. (2021), "Managing the distributional effects of environmental and climate policies: The narrow path for a triple dividend", *OECD Environment Working Papers* 188. [151]

Wakefield, S. and J. Baxter (2010), "Linking health inequality and environmental justice: Articulating a precautionary framework for research and action", *Environmental Justice*, Vol. 3/3, https://doi.org/10.1089/env.2009.0044. [137]

Waldron, I. (2018), *There's something in the water : environmental racism in indigenous and black communities.* [15]

Walker, C. and J. Baxter (2017), "Procedural justice in Canadian wind energy development: A comparison of community-based and technocratic siting processes", *Energy Research and Social Science*, Vol. 29, https://doi.org/10.1016/j.erss.2017.05.016. [180]

Walker, G. (2012), *Environmental Justice: Concepts, Evidence and Politics*, https://doi.org/10.4324/9780203610671. [1]

Wang, X. et al. (2021), "Community Pressure and the Spatial Redistribution of Pollution: The Relocation of Toxic-Releasing Facilities", *Journal of the Association of Environmental and Resource Economists*, Vol. 8/3, https://doi.org/10.1086/711656. [166]

Wang, X. and K. Lo (2021), *Just transition: A conceptual review*, https://doi.org/10.1016/j.erss.2021.102291. [55]

Watkins, E. et al. (2019), "Policy Approaches to Incentivise Sustainable Plastic Design", *OECD Environment Working Papers* 149. [188]

Watkins, S. and E. Gerrish (2018), "The relationship between urban forests and race: A meta-analysis", *Journal of Environmental Management*, Vol. 209, https://doi.org/10.1016/j.jenvman.2017.12.021. [106]

Wesselink, A. et al. (2011), "Rationales for public participation in environmental policy and governance: Practitioners' perspectives", *Environment and Planning A*, Vol. 43/11, https://doi.org/10.1068/a44161. [179]

White House (2023), *Executive Order on Revitalizing Our Nation's Commitment to Environmental Justice for All*, https://www.whitehouse.gov/briefing-room/presidential-actions/2023/04/21/executive-order-on-revitalizing-our-nations-commitment-to-environmental-justice-for-all/ (accessed on 23 April 2024). [13]

White House (2021), *Executive Order on Tackling the Climate Crisis at Home and Abroad*, https://www.whitehouse.gov/briefing-room/presidential-actions/2021/01/27/executive-order-on-tackling-the-climate-crisis-at-home-and-abroad/ (accessed on 23 April 2024). [12]

White House (1994), *Executive Order 12898 of February 11, 1994 Federal Actions To Address Environmental Justice in Minority Populations and Low-Income Populations*, https://www.archives.gov/files/federal-register/executive-orders/pdf/12898.pdf. [201]

WHO (2016), *Preventing disease through healthy environments. A global assessment of the burden of disease from environmental risks*, https://iris.who.int/bitstream/handle/10665/204585/9789241565196_eng.pdf?sequence=1. [125]

WHO (n.d.), *Social determinants of health*, https://www.who.int/health-topics/social-determinants-of-health#tab=tab_1 (accessed on 23 April 2024). [195]

Whyte, K. (2017), "The recognition paradigm of environmental injustice", in *The Routledge Handbook of Environmental Justice*, https://doi.org/10.4324/9781315678986-10. [44]

Wild, C. (2012), *The exposome: From concept to utility*, https://doi.org/10.1093/ije/dyr236. [134]

Wolch, J., J. Byrne and J. Newell (2014), "Urban green space, public health, and environmental justice: The challenge of making cities 'just green enough'", *Landscape and Urban Planning*, Vol. 125, https://doi.org/10.1016/j.landurbplan.2014.01.017. [145]

Wolsink, M. (2007), *Wind power implementation: The nature of public attitudes: Equity and fairness instead of 'backyard motives'*, https://doi.org/10.1016/j.rser.2005.10.005. [174]

Wolverton, A. (2009), "Effects of socio-economic and input-related factors on polluting plants' location decisions", *B.E. Journal of Economic Analysis and Policy*, Vol. 9/1, https://doi.org/10.2202/1935-1682.2083. [103]

World Bank Group and World Trade Organization (2015), *The role of trade in ending poverty*, https://www.wto.org/english/res_e/booksp_e/worldbankandwto15_e.pdf. [79]

World Justice Project (2023), *Disparities, Vulnerability, and Harnessing Data for People-Centered Justice*, https://worldjusticeproject.org/our-work/research-and-data/wjp-justice-data-graphical-report-ii. [184]

Xepapadeas, A. (2011), *The economics of non-point-source pollution*, https://doi.org/10.1146/annurev-resource-083110-115945. [72]

Zota, A. and B. Shamasunder (2017), "The environmental injustice of beauty: framing chemical exposures from beauty products as a health disparities concern", *American Journal of Obstetrics and Gynecology*, Vol. 217/4, https://doi.org/10.1016/j.ajog.2017.07.020. [115]

## Notes

[1] The study conducted by (United States General Accounting Office, 1982[196]) galvanised the movement by empirically substantiating the concerns over environmental racism (United States Environmental Protection Agency, 2023[203]).

[2] Executive Order 12898 on Federal Actions to Address Environmental Justice in Minority Populations and Low-Income Populations (White House, 1994[201]).

[3] See (United States Environmental Protection Agency, 2023[203]) for an overview of history of environmental justice movements in the US.

[4] Executive Order 14008 on Tackling Climate Crisis at Home and Abroad (White House, 2021[12]).

[5] Executive Order 14096 on Revitalizing Our Nation's Commitment to Environmental Justice for All (White House, 2023[13]).

[6] Convention on Access to Information, Public Participation in Decision-making and Access to Justice in Environmental Matters (UNECE, 1998[46]).

[7] For instance, Article 5 requires public authorities to make environmental information "effectively" accessible for the public (Bell and Carrick, 2017[19]).

[8] However, it is recognised that data collection in some instances can help prevent and redress inequalities. For instance, the COVID-19 demonstrated that health statistics could not be fully disaggregated by ethnic origin, preventing targeted approach to protect the over-exposed groups (European Commission, 2021[200]). There are ongoing regional efforts at the European Commission and some guidance for data collection, providing guiding principles in accordance with the human-rights approach to data underpinned by "doing no harm" principle (OHCHR, 2018[205]).

[9] For instance, the region is reportedly home to the highest number of threats and (fatal) attacks on environmental defenders in the last decade (Global Witness, 2022[204]).

[10] Chemical and industrial waste caused air, ocean and river contamination and led to localised onsets of diseases such as asthma (air pollution) and bone pain (cadmium exposure) (Fan and Chou, 2017[30]).

[11] Country is a term used often to denote the lands, waterways and seas to which Aboriginal peoples are connected (Australian Institute of Aboriginal and Torres Strait Isander Studies, n.d.[194]).

[12] Disability is one example of such generalisation. For instance, reducing disability into a single category without consideration of the linguistic identity of deaf populations can create barriers for their participation (Charles and Thomas, 2007[192]).

[13] For instance, a study finds that consumption-based emissions of the wealthiest (top 1%) are larger than the emissions of those living in poverty (bottom 50%) (Bruckner et al., 2022[53]).

[14] Labour dimension of just transition remains salient in policy discussions. The preamble of the Paris Agreement features the concept, noting the need of "a just transition of the workforce and the creation of decent work and quality jobs" (UNFCCC, 2015[197]).

[15] This may reflect, for instance, the presence of high-value assets influencing the result of cost-benefit analysis and subsequent policy implementation (Hallegatte et al., 2020[61]).

[16] The World Health Organisation (WHO) describes the social determinants of health as factors other than those that are medical-related that influence health outcomes. This includes the conditions in which people are born, live and work as well as the broader context that shapes the conditions of their daily life. The

social determinants of health influence both the health of individuals as well as their access to health services. Environment broadly defined as living conditions, along with housing and basic amenities, is often identified as one of the social determinants of health that results in avoidable health inequities (WHO, n.d.[195]).

17 Despite difficulty measuring the quantity of NPS pollution and its variability over time, estimates suggest that it can constitute a large proportion of water pollution. (Hu and Huang, 2014[190]) estimate that NPS pollution constituted more than 80% of pollution in the Siheshui watershed between 2008 and 2010. Likewise, (Lee et al., 2015[189]) estimated the figure to be approximately 69% in four major watersheds in Korea.

18 Watersheds are areas where all the water that accumulates in an area through rain or snow, drains to a common body of water.

19 Persons with disabilities are estimated to face up to four times higher mortality than persons without disabilities, due to factors such as access to information and early warning systems and transportation (Stein and Stein, 2022[92]).

20 Examples include additives used in plastics products such as BPA. The use of these additives in food products can be regulated through bans and phase-out, as has been done in some countries and the European Commissions (Watkins et al., 2019[188]).

21 For instance, dark skinned women can be exposed to more chemicals through their use of personal care products such as skin-lightening creams (Zota and Shamasunder, 2017[115]).

22 Citizen science involves volunteers in the process of a scientific investigation, such as identifying research questions, conducting observations, analysing data, and using the resulting knowledge (OECD, 2022[172]) and is often carried outside professional settings, such as universities (Haklay and Francis, 2017[191]).

23 There are existing inequities in health outcomes. For instance, research consistently finds that education is linked to a number of poor health behaviours including smoking. Low-income groups are also less likely to seek medical care, in particular specialised services, across countries (OECD, 2019[199]).

24 Disease burden refers to the impact of a disease on a population, measured in disability-adjusted life years (DALYs) (WHO, 2016[125]).

25 For instance, these cumulative impacts refer to "the totality of exposures to combinations of chemical and non-chemical stressors and their effects on health, well-being, and quality of life outcomes." (United States Environmental Protection Agency, 2022[202]).

26 For a review of empirical literature on the impact of various environmental (dis)amenities on housing values, see (OECD, 2022[146]).

27 For instance, (Bento, Freedman and Lang, 2015[193]) find that the rent increase is half the size of the increase observed for house values.

28 For instance, projections suggest that skills such as interpersonal communications and the use of digital technologies will grow most between 2019 – 2030 (OECD, 2023[156]).

29 There may also be indirect cost arising from higher price of electricity that is used as an intermediate good to produce consumer-facing goods (Bento, 2013[153]).

30 Other important considerations include environmental impacts (e.g. on biodiversity) of this renewable infrastructure. For review, see (OECD, 2024[198]).

# 3 National approaches to environmental justice in practice

This chapter provides a high-level overview of national approaches to environmental justice based on an analysis of the responses to the OECD Environmental Justice Survey. The chapter reports on which countries use the term environmental justice. It next examines the channels through which environmental justice is pursued, such as the legal approaches, government policies, or regulatory initiatives, as well as the level of detail in which its substantive aspects are considered in the survey responses. Finally, the chapter offers illustrative examples of approaches from around the world.

## 3.1. Use of the term environmental justice

While the underlying concerns might be broad-based, the use of the term "environmental justice" is not common among national administrations (Figure 3.1). Ten of the 25 countries used the term environmental justice; of these, four used the term internally (Chile, Germany, Mexico, Scotland), four considered environmental justice in pre-existing legislation (South Africa, South Korea,Peru, United States), one had a definition derived from the judiciary (Colombia), and another had an environmental justice bill pending enactment (Canada).

The fact that less than half of national administrations surveyed use the term may reflect their varied approaches to tackling environmental inequities. Some countries use other terms that relate to the conceptual pillars of environmental justice (distributive, procedural and recognitional justice) without explicitly using the term. In a similar vein, in addition to environmental justice, Canada also uses the term "environmental racism" reflecting the usage of the term in racial equality movements. Other countries use more descriptive phrases, for example, "environmental inequalities" in the case of France. To varying extents, these terms reflect the focus of advancing environmental justice in these countries.

### Figure 3.1. Use of the term environmental justice at the national level

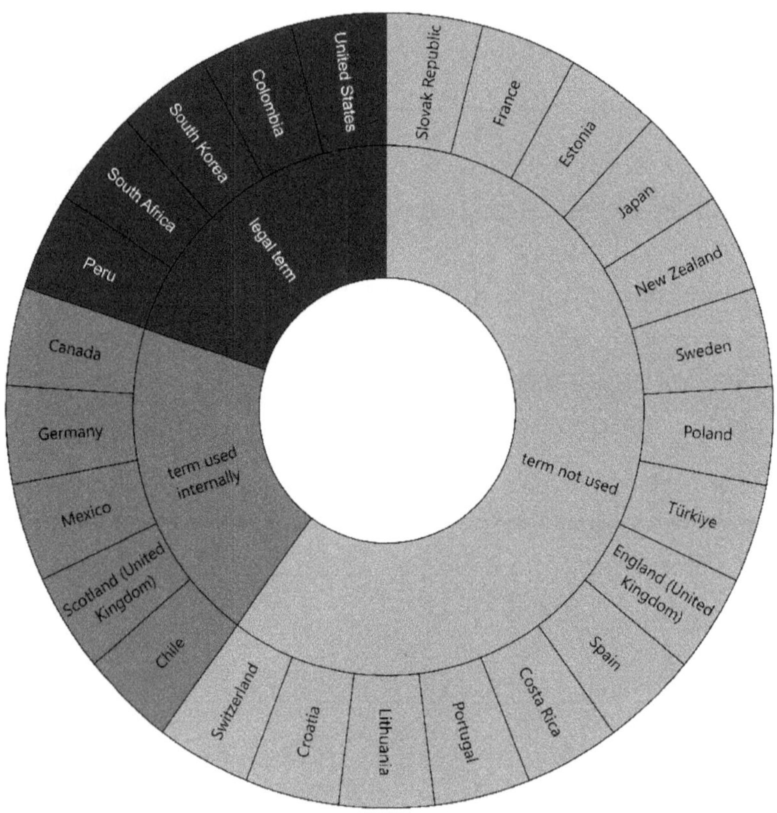


Note: Authors' review of the responses to the survey informed this classification.
Source: The OECD Environmental Justice Survey.

## 3.2. Different channels through which environmental justice is considered

Building upon the finding on the usage of the term, two categories of approaches to environmental justice were identified: *direct* approaches (those countries who use the term, and have specific measures to target environmental justice), and *indirect* approaches (those countries who do not use the term but address environmental justice in other ways, i.e., indirectly). Within the direct category, the survey identified two channels through which environmental justice is pursued: (i) legal, and (ii) policy and initiative. Likewise, within the indirect category, two channels through which environmental justice is pursued were identified: (i) added protection and safeguards, and (ii) guarantee of rights.

Environmental justice can be pursued through all these channels individually, or cumulatively; they are not necessarily mutually exclusive. For example, the United States guarantees constitutional and civil rights but also has environmental justice policies and Executive Branch directives to specifically address environmental justice through a series of executive orders. Likewise, in South Africa, environmental justice emerged as a policy principle, advancement of which became legally mandated through a legislation. Similarly, while Canada has an ongoing government initiative through their draft environmental justice legislation, rights relevant to environmental justice are still protected to some extent by guaranteeing rights; for instance, the right to a healthy environment contained within the Environmental Protection Act.

Direct approaches can be thought of as being more targeted than indirect approaches because they have a specific mandate for pursuing environmental justice (Figure 3.2). Under direct approaches, legal measures can be seen as a firmer commitment to environmental justice than statements of policy because they are less prone to change with government priorities, and they can establish enforceable rights and duties.

**Figure 3.2. Direct and indirect approaches to environmental justice and their channels**

| | | Channel targeting environmental justice (EJ) |
|---|---|---|
| Direct | Legal | EJ legislation or judicial precedent |
| | | EJ is defined explicitly |
| | | Strong legal mandate to address EJ |
| | Policy and initiative | Forthcoming legislation directly targeting EJ |
| | | Ongoing policy explicitly targeting EJ |
| | | Official documents setting out objectives targeting EJ |
| | | Other ongoing initiatives to promote EJ |
| Indirect | Added protection and safeguards | Potentially vulnerable groups recognised by other laws |
| | | Potentially vulnerable groups recognised by other policies |
| | | Detailed treatment of EJ-relevant aspects in impact assessment |
| | Guarantee of rights | Rule of law upheld and rights to recourse established |
| | | Right to healthy environment promoted |
| | | Procedural safeguards (e.g. consultation) in policy process present |
| | | Limited recognition of especially vulnerable groups |

Note: Authors' review of the responses to the survey informed this classification. The channels identified are not exhaustive and discreet.
Source: The OECD Environmental Justice Survey.

The analysis also looked at whether the substantive concerns addressed within environmental justice identified in Chapter 2[1] are considered and at what level of detail (Figure 3.3). As this characterisation entails a degree of judgement, the level of detail in which an aspect of environmental justice was considered in a survey response was assessed against pre-defined criteria. Specifically, "detailed" consideration requires that the response was explicitly focused, extensively described, or addressed differentiated impacts across the issues among other factors. Unless the response to the Survey described how it overlapped with environmental justice concerns, approaches that relate exclusively to climate policies and strategies for just transition[2] were characterised as "general". While recognising the complementarity of these concepts (see Section 2.3.4 in Chapter 2), the analysis focussed on identifying explicit references to environmental justice, due to its comprehensive perspective and limited consideration in policy to date.

Overlaying this detail-based categorisation upon the direct and indirect approaches reveals that all countries surveyed address – directly or indirectly – environmental justice concerns, albeit to varying extents. However, the analysis finds that countries which deploy direct approaches consider the substantive environmental justice concerns and do so in greater detail. Countries which deploy indirect approaches tend to consider environmental justice concerns more generally, through less targeted measures.

**Figure 3.3. Consideration of environmental justice concerns by approaches and by country**

| Approach | Category | Country | Environmental Justice: Inequitable exposure to environmental hazards and access to amenities | Environmental Justice: Inequitable distribution of the costs and benefits of environmental policy | Environmental Justice: Barriers to environmental information and participation in decision-making |
|---|---|---|---|---|---|
| Direct | Legal | **United States** | Detailed | Detailed | Detailed |
| Direct | Legal | **Colombia** | Detailed | General | Detailed |
| Direct | Legal | **South Africa** | Detailed | General | Detailed |
| Direct | Legal | **South Korea** | Detailed | General | Detailed |
| Direct | Legal | **Peru** | General | General | Detailed |
| Direct | Policy and initiative | **Canada** | Detailed | General | Detailed |
| Direct | Policy and initiative | **Mexico** | Detailed | No | Detailed |
| Direct | Policy and initiative | **Chile** | Detailed | General | General |
| Direct | Policy and initiative | **Scotland** (United Kingdom) | General | General | Detailed |
| Direct | Policy and initiative | **Germany** | Detailed | No | General |
| Indirect | Added protection and safeguards | **France** | Detailed | General | General |
| Indirect | Added protection and safeguards | **New Zealand** | General | General | Detailed |
| Indirect | Added protection and safeguards | **Switzerland** | General | General | General |
| Indirect | Added protection and safeguards | **England** (United Kingdom) | General | General | General |
| Indirect | Guarantee of rights | **Japan** | General | General | General |
| Indirect | Guarantee of rights | **Sweden** | General | General | General |
| Indirect | Guarantee of rights | **Poland** | General | General | General |
| Indirect | Guarantee of rights | **Portugal** | General | General | General |
| Indirect | Guarantee of rights | **Costa Rica** | General | No | General |
| Indirect | Guarantee of rights | **Spain** | No | General | General |
| Indirect | Guarantee of rights | **Estonia** | General | No | General |
| Indirect | Guarantee of rights | **Croatia** | General | No | General |
| Indirect | Guarantee of rights | **Lithuania** | No | General | General |
| Indirect | Guarantee of rights | **Slovak Republic** | No | General | No |

● Detailed consideration
● General consideration
○ No consideration

Note: The level of details considered is categorised by authors based on the review of survey responses. Türkiye and the European Commission were not classified as their responses considered more sectoral issues which hindered the assessment of their coverage of the three substantive environmental justice concerns.
Source: The OECD Environmental Justice Survey.

This finding may reflect the competing advantages and disadvantages of different channels for pursuing environmental justice, along with the varying salience of different environmental justice concerns across countries. All approaches to environmental justice have their relative advantages and disadvantages. Guaranteeing rights plays a role in promoting environmental justice. Additionally, poor environmental quality can negatively impact an array of rights; such as to health, or adequate living standards. More practically, enforcement mechanisms for such rights – embodied in legal systems – provide routes to recourse for the victims of environmental injustice (Lewis, 2012[1]).[3]

However, one limitation of rights-based approaches is that mandating equal rights does not necessarily recognise *ex ante* that some groups are more vulnerable to poor environmental quality and that such groups may also face barriers to accessing legal recourse. Added protection and safeguards might enable corrective measures to address these inequities. Yet, such approaches, in some instances, can still be reactionary which may limit their effectiveness of identifying less well recognised vulnerabilities in favour of the most high-profile issues in a given context.

Accordingly, environmental justice policies explicitly targeting or taking into account vulnerable groups may be preferable in recognition of these potential problems. However, while policies and initiatives play an important role in influencing environmental justice outcomes, they are typically held to a lower standard of accountability than laws which create binding obligations upon specific actors alongside enforcement mechanisms (United Nations Development Programme, 2022[2]). Consequently, legal protections and requirements that go beyond purely rights-based approaches may be appropriate in some cases.

## 3.3. Examples of direct approaches across countries

### *3.3.1. Legal approaches to environmental justice*

Uniquely, the United States has strengthened its agenda on environmental justice through a series of executive orders.[4] A 2023 Executive Order[5] defines environmental justice as: "the just treatment and meaningful involvement of all people, regardless of income, race, colour, national origin, Tribal affiliation, or disability, in agency decision-making and other Federal activities that affect human health and the environment" (White House, 2023[3]) (see Box 3.1 for the full definition). The United States' definition reflects the three aspects of environmental justice discussed in Chapter 2, and Executive Orders 12898 and 14096 provide clear directives for federal agencies to advance environmental justice. For instance, a 1994 Executive Order[6] directed federal agencies to: "identify and address the disproportionately high and adverse human health or environmental effects of their actions on minority and low-income populations, to the greatest extent practicable and permitted by law" and mandated developing a strategy for implementing environmental justice (United States Environmental Protection Agency, 2023[4]). This study also finds that the United States is the only country to provide a detailed consideration of the distributive effects of environmental policies.

In Colombia, the Constitutional Court has opined that environmental justice is composed of four elements found in the 1991 constitution, which have also been complied in constitutional jurisprudence with reference to the definition developed by the US EPA. [7] In a ruling, both participatory and distributive dimensions of environmental justice were acknowledged. The case concerned the environmental degradation suffered by the Indigenous communities of the Zenú People because of the construction of the Cantagallo landfill near their residence. The court found that the defendants – which were national and local environmental authorities, a public utility company, and the Colombian Ministry of Interior – had violated various rights of the plaintiffs. For instance, these violations included right to prior consultation of those affected as part of the permitting process, as well as recognition of the plaintiffs Indigeneity by non-acceptance of their presence in the area where the landfill was built. Additionally, in a 2019 ruling concerning the failure to consult a predominantly Black community in Playa Blanca about removal of marine access rights to a vital area,[8] the Colombian constitutional court grounded its definition of environmental justice in principles established within its constitutional jurisprudence such as sustainability and the precautionary principle.

Colombia's survey response indicates that it considers the inequitable distribution of environmental harms and benefits as well as participation and engagement in detail. For example, Colombia cited various measures that facilitate public participation such as a decree[9] of the Colombian government "to adopt the Public Policy on Citizen Participation [...]", and their "National Development Plan" which aims to create an "Escazú Inter-institutional Commission" to strengthen environmental safeguards. Colombia's response also confirmed that the right to prior consultation is understood as a protection of environmental justice for Indigenous or Tribal Peoples (Gobierno de Colombia, 2023[5]). Regarding the distributional impact of environmental policies, while the principle of "distributive justice" was mentioned, there was no substantive consideration beyond highlighting its importance. This may reflect the fact that the development of environmental justice was driven by the judiciary in Colombia. [10]

South Africa's approach to environmental justice is rooted in the Bill of Rights contained in the post-apartheid Constitution of 1996 (Government of South Africa, 1996[6]). The concept of environmental justice was first specifically defined in the principles of the 1998 National Environmental Policy White Paper, which makes it a responsibility for the government to "integrate environmental considerations with social, political and economic justice and development in addressing the needs and rights of all communities, sectors and individuals" to redress environmental injustices, both past and present (Department of Forestry, Fisheries and the Environment, 1998[7]). The principle of environmental justice was further mandated by the National Environmental Management Act (NEMA) (Government of South Africa, 1998[8]).

Notably, the right to participation in environmental decision-making is also operationalised in NEMA section 2.4(f), which recognises that people must have "the opportunity to develop the understanding, skills and capacity necessary for achieving equitable and effective participation" (*ibid*). Building on this legislation, the judiciary in South Africa has also played an active role in the development of jurisprudence on what constitutes meaningful public participation (Hall and Lukey, 2023[9]). For instance, in a case concerning the exploration right for oil and gas,[11] the Court declared that some of the procedural aspects of the public consultation, including the notice published only in Afrikaans and English[12] and the location of public meetings far from the affected communities, were flawed.

In South Korea, environmental justice finds its concrete expression in the Article 2 of the Framework Act on Environmental Policy. A number of plans ensued to operationalise the concept in policymaking, with the "Comprehensive Plan for National Environment 2020-2040" aiming to develop a framework for promoting environmental justice and conduct an evaluative work on the current situation by 2030 (Ministry of Environment, 2019[10]) and Comprehensive Environmental Justice Plan (2020-2024) outlining the implementation. Specific communities and groups at risk of environmental justice concerns are also identified in the Environmental Health Act, such as those residing near industrial complexes and in densely populated areas, as well as those particularly susceptible to exposure to environmental hazards, including children and pregnant women (Korea Legislation Research Institute, 2008[11]).

The Peruvian approach to environmental justice is premised on its procedural aspects, access to legal recourse in particular, with Article IV (right of access to environmental justice) of the General Environmental Law highlighting the right to quick, simple and effective action before the administrative and jurisdictional entities as well as due protection of people's health.[13] Another noteworthy aspect of the Law is the equity principle, stipulating the requirement for environmental policies to contribute to "eradicating poverty and reducing the prevailing social and economic inequities, as well as to the sustainable economic development of the disadvantaged populations" (Ministry of Environment of Peru, 2005[12]). Furthermore, in addition to consideration for vulnerable groups such as Indigenous Peoples, particular emphasis is placed on the protection of environmental defenders through the Sectoral Protocol for the Protection of Environmental Defenders which aims to guarantee their rights and establishes a range of preventive and protective measures (Ministry of Environment of Peru, 2021[13]).

These five cases demonstrate that environmental justice can be advanced through all three branches of government. Just as the United States shows the executive branch of government can play an important role in driving environmental justice forward, Colombia and South Africa exemplify that the judiciary can also be a key lever. Moreover, a crucial aspect of both the Colombian cases cited above was recognition of the right of Indigenous Peoples to free, prior and informed consultation, which could have future implications for a broader public participation in environmental decision-making. This may reflect that Colombia is a signatory[14] to the Escazú Agreement which highlights the role of international instruments in establishing the rights which are foundational to environmental justice.

Finally, the examples of South Africa, South Korea and Peru highlight the role of legislatures, which solidify environmental protection by creating legal standards which identify citizens' rights and the actors responsible for upholding them (UNDP, 2022[14]). Instead of having one dedicated environmental justice law, the principle of environmental justice is operationalised in varied broader environmental legislation which provide a legal basis for addressing the issues through implementation of policy and jurisprudence. For instance, in the case of South Korea, the legal basis founded in the Framework Act on Environmental Policy prompted the development of the Comprehensive Environmental Justice Plan 2020-2024.

Reflecting the locally specific concerns, these acts of legislation place varying weight on the aspects of environmental justice. While in South Africa, the emergence of environmental justice coincided with a wave of democratic change and the need to redress the historical legacy of racism and apartheid, in South Korea the process was motivated by the industrial pollution and its health impact during the period of rapid yet regionally uneven economic growth (OECD, 2017[15]). Peru's emphasis on procedural aspects of environmental justice, seems to reflect the increasing awareness of the need to protect environmental defenders for whom their activism can constitute a threat to their lives (Article 19, 2016[16]).

### Box 3.1. Definitions of environmental justice in the United States, Colombia, South Africa, South Korea and Peru

A comparison of definitions across the five countries that deploy legal approaches to advance environmental justice is illustrative of how it is conceptualised in practice. All of the definitions contain the element of distributive environmental justice, while some also highlight procedural and recognitional environmental justice. Peru's definition, for instance, recognises the right of access to justice to address harm that are moral, rather than economic in nature.

In keeping with the origin of environmental justice, the need for corrective remedies is explicit in the United States ("legacy of racism") and South Korea ("fair compensation for losses"). Furthermore, while all countries refer to the public in its entirety ("all people", "all citizens", "any and every person"), some identify relevant categories, with the United States highlighting "income, race, color, national origin, Tribal affiliation" and Colombia noting "race, colour, national origin, culture, education and income" in particular.

#### United States and the Executive Order 14096 (2023)

> *"the just treatment and meaningful involvement of all people, regardless of income, race, color, national origin, Tribal affiliation, or disability, in agency decision-making and other Federal activities that affect human health and the environment so that people are fully protected from disproportionate and adverse human health and environmental effects (including risks) and hazards, including those related to climate change, the cumulative impacts of environmental and other burdens, and the legacy of racism or other structural or systemic barriers; and have equitable access to a healthy, sustainable, and resilient environment in which to live, play, work, learn, grow, worship, and engage in cultural and subsistence practices."*

**Colombia and the judicial rulings (Ruling T-294 of 2014 and Ruling T-021 of 2019)**

> *"the fair treatment and meaningful participation of all people regardless of race, colour, national origin, culture, education or income with respect to the development and enforcement of environmental laws, regulations and policies."*
>
> *"Environmental justice is composed of four elements found in the 1991 Constitution, which have also been compiled in constitutional jurisprudence, namely: i) distributive justice; ii) participatory justice; iii) the principle of sustainability; and iv) the precautionary principle... environmental justice identifies contexts of inequity in the distribution of environmental benefits and burdens. Together, it shows the way to re-establish the rupture of the just order through the participation of the affected collectives and the configuration of compensation or reparation measures for the ecosystem and/or environmental burdens borne. Such criteria also apply in the implementation of environmental protection measures that entail a disturbance to a vulnerable community".*

**South Africa and the National Environmental Management Act (1998)**

> *"Environmental justice must be pursued so that adverse environmental impacts shall not be distributed in such a manner as to unfairly discriminate against any person, particularly vulnerable and disadvantaged persons."*

**South Korea and the Framework Act on Environmental Policy, Article 2 (amended in 2019)**

> *"The State and local governments shall endeavour to realise environmental justice by ensuring all citizens' substantial participation in the enactment or amendment of environmental statutes, regulations, ordinances and rules or the formulation or implementation of policies, access to information about environment, equitable sharing of environmental benefits and burdens, and fair compensation for losses caused by environmental pollution or environmental damage.*

**Peru and the General Environmental Law, Article 4 (2005)**

> *"Right of access to environmental justice: Every person has the right to a quick, simple and effective action before the administrative and jurisdictional entities, in defence of the environment and its components, ensuring the due protection of the health of people individually and collectively, the conservation of biological diversity, the sustainable use of natural resources, as well as the conservation of the cultural heritage linked to them. Legal actions may be filed even in cases where the economic interest of the plaintiff is not affected. The moral interest legitimizes the action even when it does not directly refer to the plaintiff or his family".*

Source: (White House, 2023[3]), (Corte Constitucional de Colombia, 2014[17]), (Corte Constitucional de Colombia, 2019[18]), (Government of South Africa, 1998[8]), (Korea Legislation Research Institute, 2019[19]), (Ministry of Environment of Peru, 2005[12]).

### *3.3.2. Environmental justice policies and initiatives*

Canada currently has draft legislation[15] centred upon environmental justice. Related policy documents identify the importance of procedural, recognitional, and distributive justice. The draft legislation also addresses both inequitable exposure to environmental harms and participation and engagement in detail. Indeed, once developed, Canada's "Environmental Justice Strategy" aims to address the "link between race, socio-economic status and exposure to environmental risk." (Prime Minister of Canada, 2021[20]).

Discussion of the distributional impacts of environmental policies was less detailed in Canada's response. It noted that, policymakers in Canada use a "Gender Based Analysis (GBA) Plus" tool for this purpose which considers the impact of policies upon various geographical, cultural, and socio-economic aspects. The GBA Plus tool is applied generally to all policies and is comparable to impact assessment methodologies deployed in other countries.[16] While standardised guidance for assessing the distributive impacts of policies does address their inequitable impacts *ex ante*, there remains potential for follow-up measures that prevent unforeseen distributional problems *ex post* and for measures targeted at environmental impacts more specifically.

The German Environment Agency conducts policy research and develops recommendations for policymakers at the federal, state, and municipal levels on methods of enhancing environmental justice in various municipalities. Germany's Environment Agency defines environmental justice as "reducing and avoiding the socio-spatial concentration of health-related environmental burdens and ensuring fair access to environmental benefits". This focus is narrower as it does not account for the participation and engagement in environmental policy or for the distributional impacts of environmental policies.[17] The German Environment Agency's approach, however, exemplifies a synergistic application of existing frameworks, such as improving planning and conservation, or engagement to promote environmental justice (Box 3.2).

### Box 3.2. German Environment Agency on addressing inequitable exposure to environmental harms in urban areas

The German Environment Agency seeks to address inequitable exposure to environmental harms in an urban context through a holistic use of existing measures such as "[...] urban and neighbourhood development concepts, landscape planning, traffic development planning, participation procedures, neighbourhood management [...]". Various examples of ways to promote urban environmental justice include:

- **Noise pollution from traffic**: using noise-reducing solutions for road surfaces/landscaped tramlines, installing soundproof windows, introducing speed limits.
- **Air pollution and urban climate**: traffic control measures, increasing green areas to promote cooling.
- **Indoor air quality:** promoting energy efficient retrofitting.
- **Green transport**: increasing the appeal of public transport, cycling, and walking.
- **Education about the environmental and health:** increasing exposure to green spaces, information provision.

This is not to say that environmental justice is necessarily adequately addressed simply by virtue of having a variety of differently targeted environmental policies in isolation from each other. Rather, the German Environment Agency emphasises that the various levers that impact the urban environment should be used synergistically so that the overall effect is greater than the sum of its parts.

Source: (German Environment Agency, 2015[21]) (German Institute of Urban Affairs, n.d.[22])

The Chilean Office of Just Socio-Ecological Transition defines environmental justice as the "[…] equitable distribution of environmental benefits and burdens in society, especially with regard to ecosystem protection, pollution prevention and mitigation of environmental impacts […]". Indeed, the Chilean government is acutely aware of the inequitable distribution of environmental harms having acknowledged especially environmentally vulnerable territories, which are Huasco, Quintero-Puchuncaví, and Coronel. These areas are termed "Sacrifice Zones" [18] due to the high levels of localised pollution and environmental hazards produced by industrial facilities.

The Scottish and Mexican governments explicitly use the term environmental justice and rely upon similar, rights-based, definitions. While the former emphasises the negative right to freedom from poor environmental quality, the latter emphasises the positive right to a healthy environment. In Scotland, although no standard definition is used, a recent report on environmental governance refers to environmental justice as follows: "It is important that everyone has the opportunity to enjoy a life free from poor environmental quality. It is also important that there are readily available routes for individuals to secure good environmental quality for themselves and their communities." (The Scottish Government, 2023[23]). In Mexico, the Secretariat of Environment and Natural Resources (SEMARNAT) defines environmental justice as "obtaining a timely legal solution to an environmental conflict, taking into account that all people must partake of the same conditions to access environmental justice" (Secretaría de Medio Ambiente y Recursos Naturales, 2020[24]). In both countries, detailed attention is paid to the importance of engagement and participation, suggesting a greater emphasis on procedural justice in these countries.

In Scotland, the "Report into the Effectiveness of Governance Arrangements" highlights the "Human Rights Bill" which recognises the right to a healthy environment as a human right and improves access to justice by providing more ways through which individuals can hold public authorities to account (The Scottish Government, 2023[23]). Moreover, in 2016 the Scottish Government consulted the public on developments in environmental justice (*ibid*).[19] The current Mexican administration places particular emphasis on promoting participation for communities and groups at risk such as Indigenous groups and Afro-Mexicans through its "Environmental Justice Provision Programme 2021-2024" (Procuraduria Federal de Proteccion al Ambiente, Gobierno de México, 2021[25]).

## 3.4. Examples of indirect approaches across countries

### *3.4.1. Added Protection and Safeguards*

The responses of the countries categorised as having added protection and safeguards to promote environmental justice indicated that their policies, laws, or procedures target particularly vulnerable groups more broadly, instead of focussing specifically on the environment. For example, England is subject to the UK Parliament's "Equality Act (2010)" which aims to reduce "[…] discrimination and harassment related to certain personal characteristics […]"[20] (The National Archives, 2010[26]). The Act applies indirectly to a variety of areas where potential discrimination could arise including in the development of environmental policy. For example, the official guidance on conducting policy appraisal – the Green Book – mandates that all impact assessments pay due regard to the Equality Act (Government of the United Kingdom, 2022[27]). While this does not target environmental justice directly, it demonstrates a detailed recognition of situations in which certain groups are more vulnerable and provides an additional legal framework for addressing their needs.

Similarly, Switzerland's regulatory impact assessment methodology ("RFA") demonstrates thorough consideration of the impacts of policies on particular groups (State Secretariat for Economic Affairs, 2022[28]). Although its response identifies fair treatment of all groups as a guiding normative principle, it recognises the need to mitigate inequities and prevent them from becoming reinforced. For instance, checkpoint three of Switzerland's "RFA" methodology explicitly asks "[…] what impact (costs, benefits, distribution effects) does the proposal have on individual social groups?". Amongst other things, the "RFA" cites education, employment, wages, and working conditions which suggests a lesser focus on categories, such as race or gender, in favour of identifying socio-economically vulnerable groups. Perhaps this divergence of emphasis between, the Swiss and, for example, US or Canadian governments, reflects the different historical origin of environmental justice in North America. Switzerland offers an example of an approach which – while not targeting environmental justice directly – provides protection for vulnerable groups through additional procedural safeguards.

Within New Zealand's regulatory impact analysis, additional safeguards are present to consider the impact on equity and disproportionate impacts on different population groups. Such recognition of vulnerability of some communities is also reflected in the requirements for consultation of Māori, mandated by many pieces of environmental legislation including National Policy Statements under the Resource Management Act 1991. In addition, Māori need to be consulted or involved in local planning processes by local government. Strengthening this mandate, the Ministry for the Environment has recently committed to "reflect the Treaty of Waitangi[21] in environmental decision-making" in its Strategic intentions (2023-2027) (Ministry for the Environment, 2023[29]). Another group that is given attention in environmental policymaking in New Zealand is the youth – a Climate Change Youth Advisory Group is contributing to the ongoing development of the second Emissions Reduction Plan, by supporting the design of engagement measures as well as providing inputs into the policy development.

Despite not using the term environmental justice explicitly, France recognises the existence of "environmental inequalities" and that some parts of the population may be more exposed to environmental risks. To reduce such risks, the "National and Regional Environmental Health Plans" were put in place to "[...] better account for the concept of the "*exposome*" (see also Section 2.4.1 in Chapter 2), all exposure to environmental hazards throughout life, with particular attention paid to populations at risk or those most exposed". Differentiated impacts on vulnerable groups are also mentioned in a report by France Stratégie, which concludes that young people living in large cities and those facing higher unemployment and poverty rates in rural and former industrial regions are particularly exposed to pollution (Fosse, Salesse and Viennot, 2022[30]). The French administration also notes that "environmental equity" is used as a guiding principle when choosing policy instruments and that gender, disability, and young age are mandatory considerations when developing policy, demonstrating some consideration of the distributional impacts of environmental policies.

### *3.4.2. Guarantee of rights*

Most countries have legislative and policy-based frameworks – often in the context of environmental rights or rights to appeal decisions of public bodies – that provide a baseline of protection for environmental justice concerns. For example, Article 2(a) of Costa Rica's "Organic Law of the Environment", number 7554, declares that the "[...] environment is the common heritage of all the inhabitants of the Nation and therefore both at the institutional level (of the Executive Branch) and at the jurisdictional level, citizens have the right to equal treatment [...]" (General Attorney of the Republic, 1995[31]). Moreover, the Costa Rican government cites the equality of persons before the law and their right to non-discrimination, Article 33 of its Constitution, as an example of the protection that applies to potentially vulnerable groups.

Similarly, the Croatian government, citing Article 38.4 of its Constitution, protects the right of citizens to access information which provides a baseline protection for procedural aspect of environmental justice. It is noteworthy that constitutional protection of rights – though not specifically targeted – provides a strong basis for the development of more targeted protection of environmental justice. Meanwhile, Japan's focus on prevention of inequitable burden seeks to ensure broad-based protection and speedy remedies through institutionalised mechanisms that were progressively strengthened against the backdrop of rapid industrial growth (Box 3.3).

## Box 3.3. Japan's preventive approach to environmental justice

### Institutional mechanisms for preventing disproportionate environmental burden

Although the term environmental justice is not used, Japan's response highlights the emphasis on prevention of inequitable exposure to environmental harms from arising in the first place. The Central Environmental Council (CEC), established in 2001, is one of the key institutional mechanisms that allows for anticipating and mitigating unintended policy consequences. The CEC, a group composed of academic experts, representatives of local governments, industrial associations, labour unions and other civil society representatives with up to 30 members, regularly meet to study and deliberate on new environmental policy. Particular consideration is given to ensure that representatives of groups affected by the policy are present. These deliberations form the basis upon which the bills are drafted and further deliberated in the Diet (legislature).

### Progressively strengthened mechanisms for prevention and speedy remedies for "*Kogai*"

Collectively known as *Kogai*, directly translating as "public harm" to characterise environmental pollution, is defined in Article 2(3) of the Basic Environment Law (1993) as "air pollution, water pollution[...], soil contamination, noise, vibration, ground subsidence and offensive odours" that affect "an extensive area as a result of business and other human activities which cause damage to human health or the living environment" (Ministry of the Environment, 1993[32]). Importantly, even if there is one victim, it is considered to affect a "broad area" as defined in the Act as long as the geographical spread is recognisable or foreseen (Ministry of Internal Affairs and Communications, n.d.[33]).

Japan's preventive approach is deeply rooted in the increased incidence of pollution that accompanied its rapid economic growth from the 1950s onward. While civil lawsuits were the primary means of resolving pollution disputes, they were insufficient for victim relief and limited the speedy and appropriate resolution of pollution disputes. This is because it was difficult to prove the causal relationship between the source of the pollution and the harms, a large amount of litigation costs were required, and it took a considerable number of years for the judgment to be final (Ministry of Internal Affairs and Communications, n.d.[34]). Against this backdrop, in order to ensure prompt and appropriate resolution of pollution disputes, the government established the Prefectural Pollution Review Board in each prefecture and the Environmental Dispute Coordination Commission in the national government to address pollution disputes, in addition to judicial resolution by the courts, based on the Act on the Settlement of Environmental Pollution Disputes. These Board and Commission are independent in resolving disputes according to their respective jurisdictions but cooperate with each other through the exchange of information to ensure the smooth operation of the system. In addition to these organisations, each prefecture and municipality has its own pollution complaint consultation office for the prompt and appropriate resolution of pollution complaints (Ministry of Internal Affairs and Communications, n.d.[33]). Thus, the government has taken responsibility of proactively addressing environmental harms, resulting in progressively more preventative approach over time.

For large-scale issues, the national government has readily committed to supporting local government. A prominent example is the case of illegal dumping of toxic industrial wastes in *Teshima* island, which has resulted in contamination of soil and groundwater by hazardous substances in late 1970s (Takatsuki, 2003[35]). The government has enacted supporting measures to the local authorities by playing a liaising role for local authorities and local residents through mediation procedures, as well as enacting necessary legislation, and making public funds available for the waste treatment.

## 3.5. Key insights

Most countries do not directly target environmental justice *per se* but do so indirectly through a variety of other related measures. The ways in which countries address environmental justice directly also vary and can entail all three branches of government. Likewise, indirect approaches to environmental justice differ; some countries protect environmental justice by guaranteeing rights to all, whereas others provide additional protection to vulnerable groups through safeguards such as anti-discrimination law or detailed impact assessment methodologies.

Rights-based approaches provide an important baseline consisting of procedural and substantive rights that are important for experiencing a healthy environment. These might include the rights to equal protection of the law, to participate in the conduct of government and public affairs, and to seek, receive and impart information. While the case of Colombia shows how such a baseline can be utilised to protect environmental justice, there is an intermediate step in this process – the judiciary. In such cases, a grievance must already have arisen for the right to gain further protection, and there are often barriers to engagement in such legal processes. Supplementary measures could promote environmental justice *ex ante* – for example through policies, initiatives, or more targeted law that positively mandate stronger protection of environmental justice. They can also strengthen and enable the legal basis for rectifying existing practices that are considered unjust (Agyeman, Bullard and Evans, 2002[36]).

There is a clear relationship between direct approaches to environmental justice and greater detail of coverage of the three substantive aspects environmental justice concerns. Countries that deploy direct approaches consider all three dimensions of environmental justice and do so in greater detail. The countries that deploy indirect approaches tend to consider environmental justice concerns more generally, through less targeted measures.

Another key insight from this analysis is that there is widespread focus upon both inequitable exposure to environmental hazards and amenities, as well as barriers to information and participation in environmental decision-making. However, consideration of the inequitable distribution of the costs and benefits of environmental policy is a relative blind-spot in country approaches to environmental justice.

## References

Agencia Peruana de Noticias (2018), *Justicia Ambiental: estos son los 10 compromisos del Pacto en Madre de Dios*, https://andina.pe/agencia/noticia-justicia-ambiental-estos-son-los-10-compromisos-del-pacto-madre-dios-696792.aspx (accessed on 23 April 2024). [46]

Agyeman, J., R. Bullard and B. Evans (2002), "Exploring the Nexus: Bringing together sustainability, environmental justice and equity", *Space and Polity*, Vol. 6/1, https://doi.org/10.1080/13562570220137907. [36]

Article 19 (2016), *A Deadly Shade of Green. Threats to Environmental Human Rights Defenders in Latin America*, https://www.article19.org/data/files/Deadly_shade_of_green_A5_72pp_report_hires_PAGES_PDF.pdf. [16]

Corte Constitucional de Colombia (2019), *Sentencia T-021/19*, https://www.corteconstitucional.gov.co/relatoria/2019/T-021-19.htm (accessed on 23 April 2024). [18]

Corte Constitucional de Colombia (2014), *Sentencia T-294/14*, https://www.corteconstitucional.gov.co/relatoria/2014/t-294-14.htm (accessed on 23 April 2024). [17]

Department of Forestry, Fisheries and the Environment (1998), *White Paper on Environmental Management Policy for South Africa*, https://www.dffe.gov.za/sites/default/files/legislation/2023-09/environemntal_management_0.pdf. [7]

Fairburn, J., G. Walker and G. Smith (2005), *Investigating environmental justice in Scotland: links between measures of environmental quality and social deprivation*, https://eprints.staffs.ac.uk/1828/1/1828.pdf. [39]

Fosse, J., C. Salesse and M. Viennot (2022), *Inégalités environnementales et sociales se superposent-elles ?*, https://www.strategie.gouv.fr/publications/inegalites-environnementales-sociales-se-superposent. [30]

General Attorney of the Republic (1995), *Ley Orgánica del Ambiente*, http://www.pgrweb.go.cr/SCIJ/Busqueda/Normativa/Normas/nrm_texto_completo.aspx?param1=NRTC&nValor1=1&nValor2=27738&nValor3=93505&strTipM=TC. [31]

German Environment Agency (2015), *Environmental justice in urban areas - development of practically oriented strategies and measures to reduce socially unequal distribution of environmental burdens*, https://www.umweltbundesamt.de/sites/default/files/medien/378/publikationen/umwelt_und_gesundheit_01_2015_summary.pdf. [21]

German Institute of Urban Affairs (n.d.), *Environmental Justice Toolbox*, https://www.toolbox-umweltgerechtigkeit.de/instrumente (accessed on 23 April 2024). [22]

Gobierno de Colombia (2023), *Bases del Plan Nacional de Desarrollo 2022-2026*, https://colaboracion.dnp.gov.co/CDT/portalDNP/PND-2023/2023-02-23-bases-plan-nacional-de-desarrollo-web.pdf. [5]

Government of South Africa (1998), *National Environmental Management Act 107 of 1998*, https://www.gov.za/documents/national-environmental-management-act (accessed on 23 April 2024). [8]

Government of South Africa (1996), *Constitution of the Republic of South Africa*, https://www.gov.za/documents/constitution/constitution-republic-south-africa-1996-04-feb-1997 (accessed on 23 April 2024). [6]

Government of the United Kingdom (2022), *The Green Book*, https://www.gov.uk/government/publications/the-green-book-appraisal-and-evaluation-in-central-government/the-green-book-2020 (accessed on 23 April 2024). [27]

Hall, J. and P. Lukey (2023), "Public participation as an essential requirement of the environmental rule of law: Reflections on South Africa's approach in policy and practice", *African Human Rights Law Journal*, pp. 303-332, https://doi.org/10.17159/1996-2096/2023/v23n2a4. [9]

HM Treasury (2022), *The Green Book*, https://www.gov.uk/government/publications/the-green-book-appraisal-and-evaluation-in-central-government/the-green-book-2020 (accessed on 23 April 2024). [41]

Knox, J. (2020), *Constructing the human right to a healthy environment*, https://doi.org/10.1146/annurev-lawsocsci-031720-074856. [38]

Korea Legislation Research Institute (2019), *Framework Act on Environmental Policy*, https://elaw.klri.re.kr/eng_mobile/viewer.do?hseq=62237&type=sogan&key=16 (accessed on 23 April 2024). [19]

Korea Legislation Research Institute (2008), *Environmental Health Act*, https://elaw.klri.re.kr/eng_mobile/viewer.do?hseq=56206&type=part&key=36 (accessed on 23 April 2024). [11]

Lewis, B. (2012), "Human Rights and Environmental Wrongs: Achieving Environmental Justice through Human Rights Law", *International Journal for Crime, Justice and Social Democracy*, Vol. 1/1, https://doi.org/10.5204/ijcjsd.v1i1.69. [1]

Ministerio del Interior, Gobierno de Colombia (2022), *Decreto 1535 – 04 agosto 2022 – para adoptar la Política Pública de Participación Ciudadana, y se dictan otras disposiciones*, https://www.mininterior.gov.co/normativas/decreto-1535-04-agosto-2022-para-adoptar-la-politica-publica-de-participacion-ciudadana-y-se-dictan-otras-disposiciones/ (accessed on 23 April 2024). [48]

Ministry for the Environment (2023), *Strategic intentions (2023-2027). He takunetanga rautaki 2023–2027*, https://environment.govt.nz/assets/publications/strategic-intentions-2023-27.pdf. [29]

Ministry of Environment (2019), *The 5th Comprehensive Plan for National Environment (2020-2040)*, https://www.me.go.kr/home/web/policy_data/read.do?menuId=10259&seq=7448 (accessed on 23 April 2024). [10]

Ministry of Environment of Peru (2021), *Protocolo sectorial para la protección de las personas defensoras ambientales*, https://cdn.www.gob.pe/uploads/document/file/2037171/RM.%20134-2021-MINAM%20con%20anexo%20Protocolo%20Sectorial.pdf.pdf?v=1627231168. [13]

Ministry of Environment of Peru (2005), *Ley General del Ambiente*, https://www.minam.gob.pe/wp-content/uploads/2017/04/Ley-N%C2%B0-28611.pdf. [12]

Ministry of Internal Affairs and Communications (n.d.), *Environmental Dispute Coordination Commission*, https://www.soumu.go.jp/kouchoi/english/ (accessed on 23 April 2024). [34]

Ministry of Internal Affairs and Communications (n.d.), *Kogai Towa*, https://www.soumu.go.jp/kouchoi/knowledge/how/e-dispute.html (accessed on 23 April 2024). [33]

Ministry of Justice (2023), *Te Tiriti o Waitangi - Treaty of Waitangi*, https://www.justice.govt.nz/about/learn-about-the-justice-system/how-the-justice-system-works/the-basis-for-all-law/treaty-of-waitangi/. [42]

Ministry of the Environment (1993), *The Basic Environment Law Chapter 1*, https://www.env.go.jp/en/laws/policy/basic/ch1.html (accessed on 23 April 2024). [32]

OECD (2017), *OECD Environmental Performance Reviews: Korea 2017*, OECD Environmental Performance Reviews, OECD Publishing, Paris, https://doi.org/10.1787/9789264268265-en. [15]

Parliament of Canada (2023), *An Act respecting the development of a national strategy to assess, prevent and address environmental racism and to advance environmental justice*, https://www.parl.ca/legisinfo/en/bill/44-1/c-226 (accessed on 23 April 2024). [50]

Poder Judicial del Perú (n.d.), *Pacto de Madre de Dios por la Justicia Ambiental*, https://www.pj.gob.pe/wps/wcm/connect/ambiente/others/as_justicia/as_pacto_md (accessed on 23 April 2024). [45]

Poder Judicial del Perú (n.d.), *Poder Judicial Crea Observatorio de Justicia Ambiental*, https://www.pj.gob.pe/wps/wcm/connect/ambiente/s_amb_prin/as_noticias/cs_n_observatorio_ambiental (accessed on 23 April 2024). [44]

Poustie, M. (2004), *Environmental justice in SEPA's environmental protection activities: a report for the Scottish Environment Protection Agency*, https://www.sepa.org.uk/media/163177/environmental_justice.pdf. [37]

Presidencia de la República, Gobierno de Colombia (2023), *Con llamado al Congreso para que se comprometa con pilares de justicia ambiental y social, Presidente Petro instaló nueva legislatura*, https://petro.presidencia.gov.co/prensa/Paginas/Con-llamado-al-Congreso-para-que-se-comprometa-con-pilares-de-justicia-ambi-230720.aspx (accessed on 23 April 2024). [49]

Prime Minister of Canada (2021), *Minister of Environment and Climate Change Mandate Letter*, https://www.pm.gc.ca/en/mandate-letters/2021/12/16/minister-environment-and-climate-change-mandate-letter (accessed on 23 April 2024). [20]

Procuraduria Federal de Proteccion al Ambiente, Gobierno de México (2021), *Programa de Procuración de Justicia Ambiental 2021 2024*, https://www.gob.mx/profepa/documentos/programa-de-procuracion-de-justicia-ambiental-2021-2024 (accessed on 23 April 2024). [25]

SAFLII (2022), *Sustaining the Wild Coast NPC and Others v Minister of Mineral Resources and Energy and Others (3491/2021) [2022] ZAECMKHC 55; 2022 (6) SA 589 (ECMk) (1 September 2022)*, https://www.saflii.org/za/cases/ZAECMKHC/2022/55.html. [43]

Secretaría de Medio Ambiente y Recursos Naturales (2020), *Programa Sectorial de Medio Ambiente y Recursos Naturales 2020-2024*, https://www.gob.mx/cms/uploads/attachment/file/566832/PROMARNAT-2020-2024.pdf. [24]

State Secretariat for Economic Affairs (2022), *Regulatory Impact Assessment - Checklist*, https://www.seco.admin.ch/seco/de/home/Publikationen_Dienstleistungen/Publikationen_und_Formulare/Regulierung/regulierungsfolgenabschaetzung/hilfsmittel/checkliste-rfa.html (accessed on 23 April 2024). [28]

Takatsuki, H. (2003), "The Teshima Island industrial waste case and its process towards resolution", *Journal of Material Cycles and Waste Management*, Vol. 5/1, https://doi.org/10.1007/s101630300005. [35]

The National Archives (2010), *Equality Act 2010*, https://www.legislation.gov.uk/ukpga/2010/15/introduction (accessed on 23 April 2024). [26]

The Scottish Government (2023), *Environmental governance arrangements: report*, https://www.gov.scot/publications/report-effectiveness-environmental-governance-arrangements/ (accessed on 23 April 2024). [23]

UNDP (2022), *Environmental Justice: securing our right to a clean, healthy and sustainable environment*, https://www.undp.org/publications/environmental-justice-securing-our-right-clean-healthy-and-sustainable-environment. [14]

United Nations Development Programme (2022), *Environmental Justice: Securing our right to a clean, healthy and sustainable environment*, https://www.undp.org/sites/g/files/zskgke326/files/2022-06/Environmental-Justice-Technical-Report.pdf. [2]

United Nations Human Rights Council (2022), *The right to a clean, healthy and sustainable environment: non-toxic environment*, https://documents-dds-ny.un.org/doc/UNDOC/GEN/G22/004/48/PDF/G2200448.pdf?OpenElement. [40]

United States Environmental Protection Agency (2023), *Summary of Executive Order 12898 - Federal Actions to Address Environmental Justice in Minority Populations and Low-Income Populations | US EPA.*, https://www.epa.gov/laws-regulations/summary-executive-order-12898-federal-actions-address-environmental-justice#:~:text=for%20all%20communities.-,E.O.,strategy%20for%20implementing%20environmental%20justice. (accessed on 23 April 2024). [4]

White House (2024), *Biden-□Harris Administration Finalizes Reforms to Modernize Environmental Reviews, Accelerate America's Clean Energy Future, Simplify the Process to Rebuild our Nation's Infrastructure, and Strengthen Public Engagement*, https://www.whitehouse.gov/ceq/news-updates/2024/04/30/biden-harris-administration-finalizes-reforms-to-modernize-environmental-reviews-accelerate-americas-clean-energy-future-simplify-the-process-to-rebuild-our-nations-infrastructure/ (accessed on 13 May 2024). [51]

White House (2023), *Executive Order on Revitalizing Our Nation's Commitment to Environmental Justice for All*, https://www.whitehouse.gov/briefing-room/presidential-actions/2023/04/21/executive-order-on-revitalizing-our-nations-commitment-to-environmental-justice-for-all/ (accessed on 23 April 2024). [3]

White House (1994), *Executive Order 12898 of February 11, 1994 Federal Actions To Address Environmental Justice in Minority Populations and Low-Income Populations*, https://www.archives.gov/files/federal-register/executive-orders/pdf/12898.pdf. [47]

## Notes

[1] These are: (i). distribution of exposure to environmental risks hazards and access to amenities, (ii) distribution of the benefits and costs of environmental policies and (iii) participation in environmental decision-making and access to justice and information.

[2] Responses from eight countries and the European Commission explicitly mentioned just transition.

[3] Illustratively, there are already innumerable precedents in which national courts have adjudicated on environmental rights around the world (Knox, 2020[38]).

[4] There is also a new regulation on environmental impact assessment that expressly incorporates environmental justice considerations (White House, 2024[51])

[5] Executive Order 14096, titled *Revitalizing Our Nation's Commitment to Environmental Justice for All* (White House, 2023[3]).

[6] Executive Order 12898, titled *Federal Actions to Address Environmental Justice in Minority Populations and Low-Income Populations* (White House, 1994[47]).

[7] See ruling T-294/14 (Corte Constitucional de Colombia, 2014[17]).

[8] See ruling T-021/19 (Corte Constitucional de Colombia, 2019[18]).

[9] See Decree 1535 of 4 August 2022 (Ministerio del Interior, Gobierno de Colombia, 2022[48]).

[10] However, the complementary desk research has found that the Colombian President has recently committed to establishing – through the legislature – measures that are grounded in two core pillars: social justice, and environmental justice. See (Presidencia de la República, Gobierno de Colombia, 2023[49]).

[11] Sustaining the Wild Coast NPC and Others v Minister of Mineral Resources and Energy and Others (3491/2021) [2022] ZAECMKHC 55; 2022 (6) SA 589 (SAFLII, 2022[43]).

[12] South Africa's Constitution recognises 11 languages. isiZulu or isiXhosa are commonly spoken languages in the affected communities.

[13] Highlighting Peru's focus on the procedural angle of environmental justice, it was identified in desk research that in 2017, the Peruvian judiciary launched the "Madre de Dios Pact for Environmental Justice in Peru", signed by, among others, the Ministry of Environment, and civil organisations. The Pact includes commitments to strengthen the constitutional and legal recognition of environmental rights and facilitating access to environmental justice through, among others, the establishment of the Environmental Justice Monitoring Observatory – an online platform gathering statistical information on environmental cases,

jurisprudence and regulations (Poder Judicial del Perú, n.d.[45]; Agencia Peruana de Noticias, 2018[46]; Poder Judicial del Perú, n.d.[44]).

[14] Some countries have signed but not ratified the Agreement. The Escazú Agreement has been signed by 24 countries and ratified by 16 countries as of May 13th, 2024.

[15] See Private Members Bill C-226 (44-1) titled: "An Act respecting the development of a national strategy to assess, prevent and address environmental racism and to advance environmental justice" (Parliament of Canada, 2023[50]).

[16] Such as Switzerland's "RFA-Checklist" (State Secretariat for Economic Affairs, 2022[28]) and the UK's "Green Book" (HM Treasury, 2022[41]).

[17] However, this narrower focus may reflect the fact that Germany's Environment Agency responded to the survey rather than its national administration.

[18] Although the term was initially used to describe areas that became uninhabitable due to nuclear experiments, it can be now applied to any "area where residents suffer devastating physical and mental health consequences and human rights violations as a result of living in pollution hotspots and heavily contaminated areas" – such areas were also identified in Romania, Zambia, United States and Canada (United Nations Human Rights Council, 2022[40]).

[19] Furthermore, the desk research has identified several relevant reports on environmental justice, commissioned by the Scottish government agencies. See: (Fairburn, Walker and Smith, 2005[39]), (Poustie, 2004[37]).

[20] The "Equality Act" is applicable across England, Scotland, Wales and Northern Ireland. While Wales and Northern Ireland did not submit separate responses to the OECD Survey, several principles outlined in the English response apply to Wales and Northern Ireland as well.

[21] The Te Tiriti o Waitangi, "Treaty of Waitangi" is an agreement between the British Crown and Māori chiefs in 1840 (Ministry of Justice, 2023[42]).

# 4 Identifying, assessing, and addressing environmental justice concerns

This chapter turns to the specific tools and policy measures through which countries identify, assess, and address environmental justice concerns, drawing on insights from the OECD Environmental Justice Survey. It first presents the findings on how countries identify communities, groups and regions vulnerable to environmental justice concerns. The chapter then outlines how these concerns are assessed, illustrating the variety of qualitative and quantitative tools and methodologies available. Next, various policy measures aimed at furthering environmental justice are explored. Lastly, this chapter points to the unifying challenges countries face in assessing and addressing environmental concerns.

## 4.1. Identifying environmental justice concerns

Existing literature on environmental justice suggests that certain groups and communities are or might become, disproportionately exposed to environmental hazards, experience adverse health impacts, or impacted by environmental policies. These communities and groups may also face specific barriers to participation in environmental decision making, access to environmental information, as well as legal recourse. This section explores whether and how countries identify communities and groups at risk of environmental injustice, based on the following set of questions:

> *Whether or not countries identify specific communities and groups at risk;*
>
> *What characteristics are considered relevant when identifying communities and groups at risk and what data are used to identify them;*
>
> *Whether there are regions where certain communities and groups may be particularly exposed to environmental justice concerns.*

### *4.1.1. Identifying communities and groups at risk*

The overwhelming majority of countries identify communities and groups at risk; although about half of them do so generally, rather than specifically in the context of the environment and environmental policies. The categories that are considered to identify groups and communities at risk are wide-ranging and relate both to demographic (e.g. age, gender, race), and spatial (e.g. type of municipality, proximity to certain environmental hazards) features.

There are certain characteristics that are considered relevant by most countries, including lack of access to key public services (Figure 4.1). This may reflect the fundamental importance of accessible public services as a precondition for ensuring equity. For instance, lack of access to health care faced by communities in remote areas, such as First Nations people in Australia, might prevent them from seeking medical remedies to exposure to environmental extremes such as heatwaves or floods (Mathew et al., 2023[1]). Perhaps unsurprisingly, given that many studies suggest inequitable environmental outcomes often coincide with economic deprivation, level of income is also a characteristic that is widely considered across many countries. Age is also commonly identified as a relevant characteristic. Attention given to age can be attributed to the unique vulnerabilities of children and the elderly to environmental hazards such as air pollution (Simoni et al., 2015[2]; Landrigan, Rauh and Galvez, 2010[3]).[1]

Moreover, lack of access to environmental amenities, health and disability as well as occupational sector are considered across countries. For instance, research clearly suggests that environmental amenities play an important role in attenuating environmental hazards (Massimo and Mannucci, 2018[4]). Interestingly, gender is also identified in over half of countries. The literature highlights that some gender-specific challenges, including the effects of exposure to chemicals on maternal health, may also overlap with environmental justice concerns (Giudice et al., 2021[5]; Butler, Gripper and Linos, 2022[6]).

**Figure 4.1. Characteristics relevant to identifying communities and groups at risk**

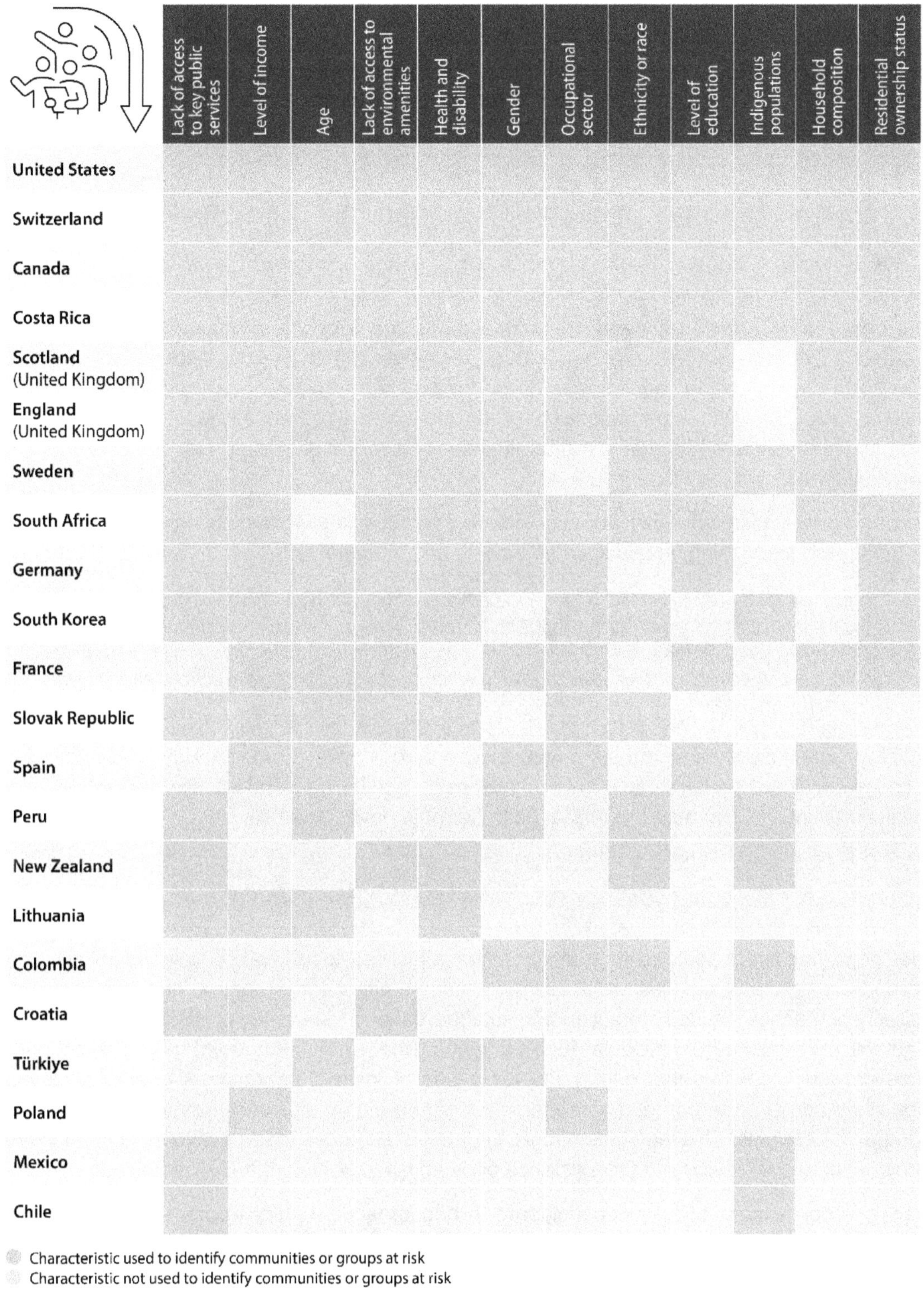


Note: Based on 22 responses. Respondents were asked to select all that apply and were invited to share other characteristics that are not available on the pre-defined list; six respondents shared such characteristics. Three characteristics are not displayed as they were selected least often; these are: Migrant status, Minority language and National origin. The data is presented from left to right in order of the highest number of countries selecting that a given characteristic is considered. While Portugal did not provide a response to this question, Japan and Estonia stated that they do not identify communities or groups at risk. The European Commission noted that all of the characteristics can be assessed in a proportionate manner.
Source: The OECD Environmental Justice Survey.

Fewer countries consider migrant status, minority language or national origin to be relevant when identifying communities and groups at risk which could be partly due to their different demographic compositions across countries. Another reason might be the lack of relevant data.[2] Nonetheless, existing research suggests that these characteristics can intersect in complex ways to create distinct vulnerabilities. The intersectionality of various characteristics in relation to environmental justice is recognised, for instance, in Brazil as described in Box 4.1.

### Box 4.1. Brazilian Committee to monitor the Black Amazon and Combat Environmental Racism

Desk research undertaken to complement the responses to the OECD Survey highlights other relevant initiatives beyond those mentioned by the survey respondents. For example, in Brazil, recognition of the link between racial inequality and environmental justice concerns prompted the use of the term "environmental racism" by policymakers, subsequently leading to the development of a dedicated initiative. The Committee to monitor the Black Amazon and Combat Environmental Racism was established in August 2023 in partnership between the Ministry of Racial Equality and the Ministry of Environment and Climate Change. The Committee's objective is to propose measures to combat environmental racism in the Amazon.

In her speech, the Minister of Racial Equality, Anielle Franco, acknowledged the intersectional character of the issue, also mentioning factors such as income and Indigeneity:

> *"No measure will be fully effective until we think about solutions by putting the most vulnerable populations at the centre, mostly poor and black people, both in rural areas and in urban centres (...) Putting our traditional peoples, quilombola communities, terreiro peoples at the forefront of protecting the Amazon is a duty not only of the Brazilian government, but of the world. It will only be possible to achieve environmental justice with racial justice".*

As environmental justice concerns cut across issues across policy domains, this inter-ministerial co-operation exemplifies how local context and challenges – advancing racial equality in Brazil – can guide the involvement of different actors in initiatives to promote environmental justice.

Source: (Secretaria de Comunicação Social, Governo do Brasil, 2024[7]), (Ministério da Igualdade Racial, Governo do Brasil, 2023[8]).

Countries deploying direct approaches to environmental justice ("legal" and "policy and initiative") tend to consider more characteristics relevant to identifying communities and groups at risk, compared to those with indirect approaches ("added protection and safeguards" and "guarantee of rights"), although there are some notable exceptions (e.g., Costa Rica, England (the United Kingdom) and Switzerland). The difference between countries that deploy the two types of indirect approaches is also observed, with countries using added protection and safeguards taking more characteristics into account than countries which guarantee of rights. This may reflect more dedicated resources made available to conduct in-depth assessments, data availability, and the existence of established bodies of anti-discrimination law.

However, a larger number of factors considered in countries with direct approaches to environmental justice may reflect the presence of salient, pre-existing environmental justice concerns. Furthermore, while consideration of vulnerabilities is critical, the breadth in characteristics considered may not necessarily translate into a more comprehensive approach to environmental justice. For instance, attempting to consider too many characteristics might spread the efforts too thin and hinder targeted measures if adequate resources are not made available.

### 4.1.2. Consideration of specific regions at a greater risk of environmental injustice

Historically, research has investigated environmental justice concerns from a spatial perspective (Walker, 2012[9]), reflecting (i) over or disproportionate representation of certain groups or communities in neighbourhoods that are underserved or overburdened with pollution and (ii) concentration of polluting industries and facilities. Often, it is a combination of these factors that puts a region at a greater risk of environmental injustice. About half of countries identify regions in which communities or groups may be particularly exposed. In the majority of the countries that identify specific regions in this context, they mirror the regions' reliance on pollution-intensive industries resulting in economic dependence as well as poor air quality. Examples include "Cancer Alley" in Louisiana, US, in which a high concentration of petrochemical companies and their toxic waste was associated with higher cancer risks for communities in primarily African American neighbourhoods (OHCHR, 2021[10]).

The regional variability of risks and its link with the sectoral composition also illustrate that the transition towards more environmentally sustainable economies may have disproportionate impacts across places, as helpfully highlighted by the concept of just transition. Specific regions in this context are identified in terms of efforts to reduce reliance on fossil fuels and carbon-intensive industries (European Commission), and the resultant transitional impact such as the closure of coal (Poland) and nuclear power plants (Spain).

In the response to the Survey, countries highlight specific regions' geographical characteristics as a relevant factor for inequitable exposure to environmental harms for various reasons. Some countries, including Scotland, consider mountainous or hilly regions and islands in relation to remoteness. Such consideration may relate to limited access to key public services, a risk factor often identified across countries. Other countries such as France, Croatia and the United States consider rural areas to be at a greater risk, for instance, due to the exposure to pollution from pesticides in agricultural land. Meanwhile, some countries consider the differential risks of regions in relation to the communities and group that reside within them. The United States and Mexico highlighted the regions inhabited by Indigenous populations, while South Africa and the Slovak Republic respectively consider urban areas with high concentration of poor and predominantly Black population[3] and settlements of marginalised Roma communities.[4]

## 4.2. Assessing environmental justice concerns

This section scans country approaches to assessing environmental justice concerns, building on the following set of questions:

> *Whether countries have specific tools (e.g. interactive maps) that allow decision-makers to combine data and information on environmental, social and economic variables;*
>
> *Whether countries use qualitative data and methods in their assessments of the risk or exposure to environmental hazards.*

### 4.2.1. Methods and tools to assess environmental justice concerns

Research in environmental justice has deployed a number of methodologies and tools, including various geographic information systems, composite indicators and screening tools to understand the spatial patterns of environmental burdens and benefits. Around half of countries have dedicated tools for assessing environmental justice concerns, such as interactive maps that allow users to combine environmental, social and economic data,[5] and an additional four countries have tools that are under development.[6] There is notable variation among countries deploying direct and indirect approaches to environmental justice, with the overwhelming majority of countries with direct approaches having or being in the process of developing such tools.[7] This might be explained by the fact that the concept is relatively more established in countries with a more direct approach, which may have afforded them more buy-in and resources to develop dedicated tools.

However, these tools tend to vary in their level of specificity for assessing environmental justice concerns. For instance, countries such as France, Canada, and Mexico have more generic data hubs and interactive maps with a range of indicators. Meanwhile, some countries have devised more dedicated assessment tools. Emerging examples suggest that it is the combination and layering of environmental, demographic and socio-economic data that deliver valuable insights. For instance, the Scottish Government has developed the "Flood Disadvantage" dataset comprising 34 vulnerability indicators, overlaying various personal, environmental (e.g. availability of green space) and social factors (e.g. income, home ownership) to map and identify communities that might be disadvantaged in terms of flood resilience and response (The Scottish Government, 2015[11]) (Box 4.2). While the Scottish Government's tool focusses on vulnerability to an environmental hazard, similar tools can also be used to examine access to environmental benefits. For instance, Natural England[8] has developed the "Green Infrastructure Map" which maps data on access to green and blue space,[9] onto socio-economic indicators (Natural England, 2021[12]).

## Box 4.2. Mapping Flood Disadvantage in Scotland (United Kingdom)

The map of Flood Disadvantage published by the Scottish Government allows for identification of communities that may be exposed to greater risks of flood due to their combined social vulnerability and geographical location. Social vulnerability is assessed based on 14 personal, environmental and social factors corresponding to three dimensions of vulnerability: sensitivity, enhanced exposure and adaptive capacity (ability to prepare, respond and recover). Combining these data, the map indicates the degree of flood disadvantage for a given area, as shown in the below figure.

### Figure 4.2. Example view of the map of Flood Disadvantage

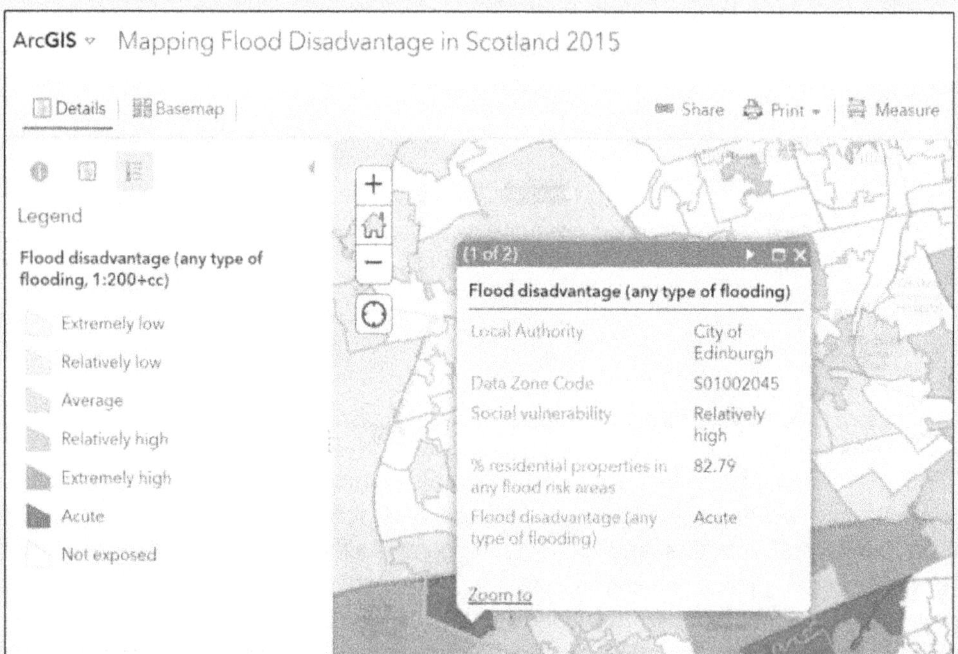


Source: (The Scottish Government, 2015[13]), (The Scottish Government, n.d.[14]).

The Environmental Justice Screening and Mapping Tool (EJScreen) developed by the US EPA, is among the most detailed tools available to identify areas of potential environmental justice concern (Box 4.3). While other tools typically focus on a single issue, the EJScreen allows for the consideration of a wider range of risks, including proximity to hazardous waste and wildfire. The tool is also built with user friendliness in mind, allowing users to generate reports and compare a set of indicators at different levels of aggregation (United States Environmental Protection Agency, n.d.[15]). Moreover, the tool allows for performing proximity analyses by inputting locations of interest and the buffer distance, providing users with spatial insights.

### Box 4.3. US EPA's Environmental Justice Screening and Mapping Tool (EJScreen)

EJScreen provides data on 13 environmental indicators (e.g. air toxics cancer risk, hazardous waste proximity) as well as seven socioeconomic ones (e.g. unemployment rate, limited English speaking) across the United States. For each of the 13 environmental indicators, an EJ index is constructed, based on the environmental indicator percentile for a given area multiplied by its demographic index. The demographic index averages the share of people of colour and low-income populations in a given area.

The supplemental index offers insight into additional dimensions of vulnerability. The Supplemental Indexes use the same methodology as the EJ Indexes, but incorporate a five-factor supplemental demographic index, as opposed to the two-factor demographic index discussed above. The supplemental demographic index averages the percent low income, percent unemployed, percent with limited English proficiency, percent with less than a high school education, and low life expectancy. Although there are certain limitations, such as availability of nationally consistent data across various environmental justice issues, it serves as a powerful means to identify priorities for further action (OECD, 2023[16]). Based on the chosen indicators, EJScreen colour-codes the selected area to visualise the degree of environmental justice concern, with the darker shades signifying greater potential environmental justice concerns (Figure 4.3).

#### Figure 4.3. Example view of the EJScreen

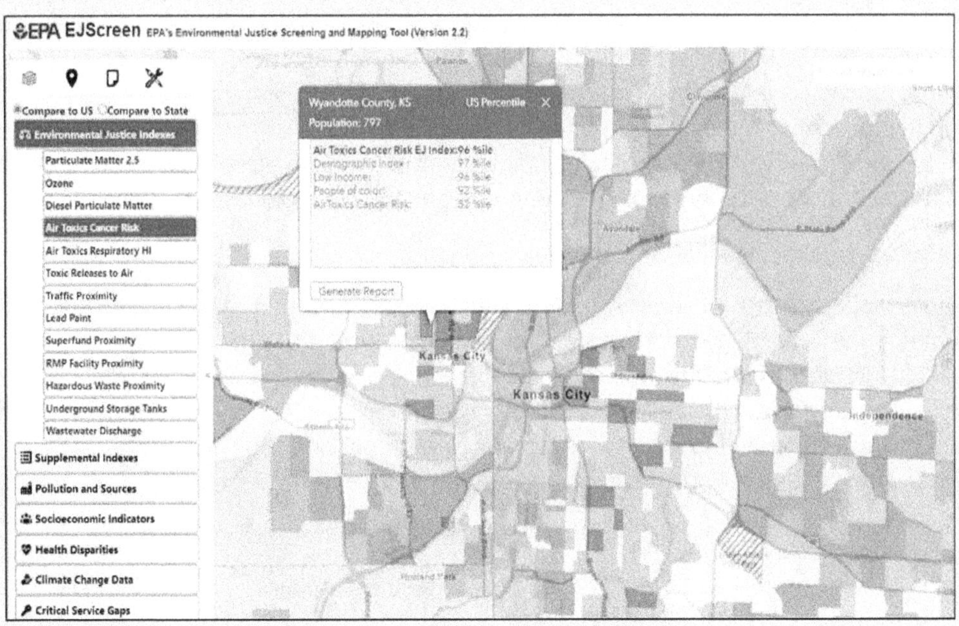


Source: (United States Environmental Protection Agency, n.d.[17]).

There are also efforts made at the sub-national level in some countries, reflecting the localised nature of environmental justice concerns. For instance, Berlin (Germany) and the City of Westminster (England, United Kingdom) have developed locally tailored tools to inform policy action.[10] Compared to tools with a national scope, they have advantages in data consistency and ability to incorporate local environmental challenges, such as noise pollution and heat islands. A comparison of the two sub-national tools also illustrates different sub-national approaches to environmental justice: the development of explicit environmental justice frameworks (Berlin) and the integration of the concept into existing strategies and solutions (The City of Westminster) (Box 4.4).

### Box 4.4. City Level Assessments: Comparison of the Berlin Environmental Justice Atlas and the Westminster Environmental Justice Measure

**Berlin Environmental Justice (EJ) Atlas (Berlin, Germany)**

The EJ Atlas was created through an inter-departmental initiative led by the State of Berlin against the backdrop of the adoption of a comprehensive environmental justice approach in the municipal environmental and health policy in Berlin. The Atlas consists of detailed maps of the city that identify the neighbourhoods that are disproportionately exposed to health-related environmental burdens. Five core environmental and social indicators are analysed: noise pollution, air pollution, bioclimatic burden, green and open spaces and social deprivation. Population density as well as quality of residential area are also available to enable additional vulnerability analysis.

**Environmental Justice Measure (The City of Westminster, England, United Kingdom)**

The City of Westminster is another local authority that has created its own environmental justice assessment tool, where the concept of environmental justice was integrated into their strategy aimed at enhancing fairness and sustainability. The Environmental Justice Measure consists of ten environmental metrics (e.g. air quality, flood risk, energy efficiency of buildings) and the existing datasets developed at a national level (socio-economic Index of Multiple Deprivation[1]).

**Similarities in approaches**

In contrast to the US EPA's EJScreen which provides multiple independent socioeconomic indicators, the tools developed by Berlin and Westminster use composite indicators of social deprivation; the Status Index in Berlin (based on unemployment, receipt of transfer payments and child poverty) and the Index of Multiple Deprivation in Westminster (based on, among others, income, employment, education as well as health and disability). The composite indicators may have an advantage of capturing the multi-dimensional character of environmental justice, as well as the ease of interpretation.

**Differences reflecting specific local concerns**

Although both tools consider air quality, heat risk and access to green and open space, some of the issues studied vary, reflecting specific local concerns and policy priorities. Unlike the EJ Atlas, the Environmental Justice Measure features an additional focus on sustainable transportation (% of people commuting by bike or walking, proximity to cycling facilities) and energy efficiency of buildings. By incorporating these elements, the tool also captures communities' ability to reduce negative environmental impacts and mitigate risks stemming from their local environment.

[1] For an overview of a different local environmental justice measure, based on the UK Index of Multiple Deprivation, see Birmingham Environmental Justice Map (Naturally Birmingham, n.d.[18]).

Source: (State of Berlin, n.d.[19]), (Senate Department for Urban Mobility, Transport, Climate Action and the Environment, n.d.[20]), (Westminster City Council, 2022[21]), (City of Westminster, 2022[22]).

While these tools can be leveraged by policymakers to identify areas of greater vulnerability or by the public to gain insights into environmental quality in their neighbourhood, similar tools are also used to better inform businesses about the potential environmental impacts of their projects. The Environmental Impact Assessment (EIA) Screening Tool developed by the South African Department of Forestry, Fisheries and the Environment enables applicants for environmental authorisation to assess environmental sensitivity of a proposed development site (Department of Forestry, Fisheries and the Environment, n.d.[23]). Depending on the location of a proposed site and the type of project (e.g. rails, pipelines, energy production, waste management facilities), the application identifies relevant EIA requirements and generates reports on the environmental sensitivity of a project. The tool uses more than 130 layers of spatial environmental sensitivity data, concerning biodiversity, agriculture, air quality priority areas or cultural heritage. Additional layers of climate change risk data, intended to provide insights into environmental justice concerns are currently under development.

Relatedly, some countries commission tailored epidemiological studies to understand the linkages between environmental quality and health outcomes for vulnerable segments of the population. For instance, Japan Environment and Children's Study, conducts a longitudinal birth cohort analysis using regularly collected biological samples and survey with an unprecedentedly large sample of 100,000 children, allowing for the identification of environmental factors affecting children's health to inform the subsequent development of appropriate risk management measures (Ministry of the Environment, Government of Japan, n.d.[24]). A similar initiative, although aimed at all age groups, is being undertaken in South Korea. Mandated by the Environmental Health Act, the National Environmental Health Survey has been conducted periodically since 2009, allowing for monitoring and measurement over time (Environmental Health Information System, n.d.[25]).

Furthermore, an analysis of the Survey revealed that over three quarters of countries employ qualitative methods in addition to quantitative ones to assess environmental justice concerns. Although the use of quantitative data and methodologies appear to be generally preferred for screening and assessing environmental justice concerns, they face important limitations due to the availability of granular data. Certain environmental justice concerns and unique lived experiences of communities may not easily lend themselves to quantification.

Importantly, engaging with the affected communities directly may also offer ways to better integrate community perspectives, culture and types of knowledge. For instance, integrating Indigenous traditional knowledge[11] can also ensure their concerns are identified and adequately assessed, mitigating the risk of climate action causing further harm to the communities (Intergovernmental Panel on Climate Change, 2023[26]). The use of qualitative methods can therefore complement quantitative data and yield additional insights. There are illustrative cases of targeted efforts to engage with the affected communities, including institutionalised mechanisms for consultations with Indigenous communities in Costa Rica (see Box 4.5), Chile, Colombia, Peru and Mexico developed in line with the Indigenous and Tribal Peoples Convention which establishes the duty of government for consulting the communities likely to be affected by legislative and administrative measures (International Labour Organization, 1989[27]).

## Box 4.5. Consultations with Indigenous communities in Costa Rica

### Costa Rica deploys a multitude of participatory and consultative mechanisms to engage with Indigenous communities

Spread over 24 territories, Indigenous Peoples make up 2.4% of the population in Costa Rica. In 2018, the General Mechanism for Consultation with Indigenous Peoples was developed together with the engagement of Indigenous communities with a purpose to represent a diverse set of cultural and spiritual worldviews (Ministry of Justice and Peace, 2018[28]). Introducing key principles and eight foundational steps, the Mechanism has been deployed to better understand the concerns of Indigenous Peoples and inform subsequent policy development for biodiversity conservation and reducing emissions from deforestation and forest degradation (REDD+).

### Biodiversity

Home to almost 6% of known species, Costa Rica's rich biodiversity provides a source for its key economic sectors including nature-based tourism and agriculture, making biodiversity conservation a policy imperative (OECD, 2023[29]). However, the introduction of protected wilderness areas (some of which overlaps with territories managed by Indigenous Peoples) have previously caused tension (*ibid*).

The National Biodiversity Management Commission (CONAGEBIO), responsible for overseeing the implementation and monitoring of the National Biodiversity Strategy 2016-2025 and Action Plan (ENB2), consists not only of civil servants, but also Indigenous Peoples, businesses and farmers. ENB2, a result-driven strategy based on over 100 targets, is an outcome of participatory processes, including Indigenous Peoples (OECD, 2023[29]). The public engagement was ensured from the very beginning of the strategy development, commencing with identification of key issues to address and sharing past experiences. One of the key achievements of the processes is a biodiversity map on ecosystem services, as well as current and future threats to them, that integrate the knowledge and values of the public. The CONAGEBIO is currently working on the application of the Indigenous consultation mechanism for two executive decrees on access to genetic and biochemical resources of biodiversity and community intellectual rights of Indigenous Peoples (CONAGEBIO, n.d.[30]).

### Reducing Emissions from Deforestation and Forest Degradation (REDD+)

The National Strategy REDD+ is foundational to Costa Rica's strategy for sustainably managing its rich forestry and contribute to increased carbon sink capacity (OECD, 2023[29]). Indigenous Peoples took an active part in its development through the National Plan for Indigenous Consultation in the Development of National REDD+ Strategy. The processes undertaken contain several novel approaches to engage meaningfully with the communities. For instance, reflecting due consideration to the unique characteristics of each Indigenous territory, the consultations were conducted at various levels of governance, with representatives from all 24 territories. Moreover, over 150 Cultural Mediators (*Mediadores Culturales*) from Indigenous communities were engaged with the authorities to exchange knowledge and disseminate information to their communities in their own language.

### There remain important challenges for promoting meaningful engagement

Despite these mechanisms and guidance on the processes, inclusive participation of the affected communities can be hindered by limited allocation of administrative and financial capacity to engage with Indigenous communities. Without adequate funding that consider these costs, it can be challenging to ensure their meaningful engagement. More targeted allocation of human and financial resources for these consultations can further foster active participation and help scale the successful examples.

## 4.3. Addressing environmental justice concerns

This section aims to identify the ways in which countries address environmental justice concerns. The findings are based on the following set of questions:

> *What measures countries have implemented specifically to address environmental justice;*
>
> *How participation and engagement in environmental policies informed any subsequent measures.*

### *4.3.1. Measures to address environmental justice concerns*

Most countries address environmental justice concerns through reducing barriers to participation in environmental decision-making (Figure 4.4). The prevalence of such measures may reflect the potential impact international instruments may have on the procedural aspect of environmental justice in national administrations. However, a cautious interpretation is required due to the sample of this survey, which includes 13 parties to the Aarhus Convention in Europe and five Latin American countries who have signed or ratified the Escazú Agreement (Chile, Colombia, Costa Rica, Mexico and Peru). Countries that are party to neither of these international conventions, such as Japan, Türkiye and the United States also implement measures to reduce barriers to participation, highlighting the broad emphasis on the procedural aspect across countries.

Reducing inequitable exposure to environmental hazards is also an important consideration across countries, with around two thirds of countries indicating they have mitigation measures in place. Meanwhile, improving access to environmental as well as economic benefits of environmental policies seem to be given less attention, with around half of countries implementing dedicated measures. Notably, the survey responses reveal that less than half of the countries address environmental justice concerns through reducing the economic costs of environmental policy.

**Figure 4.4. The use of policies to address environmental justice concerns**

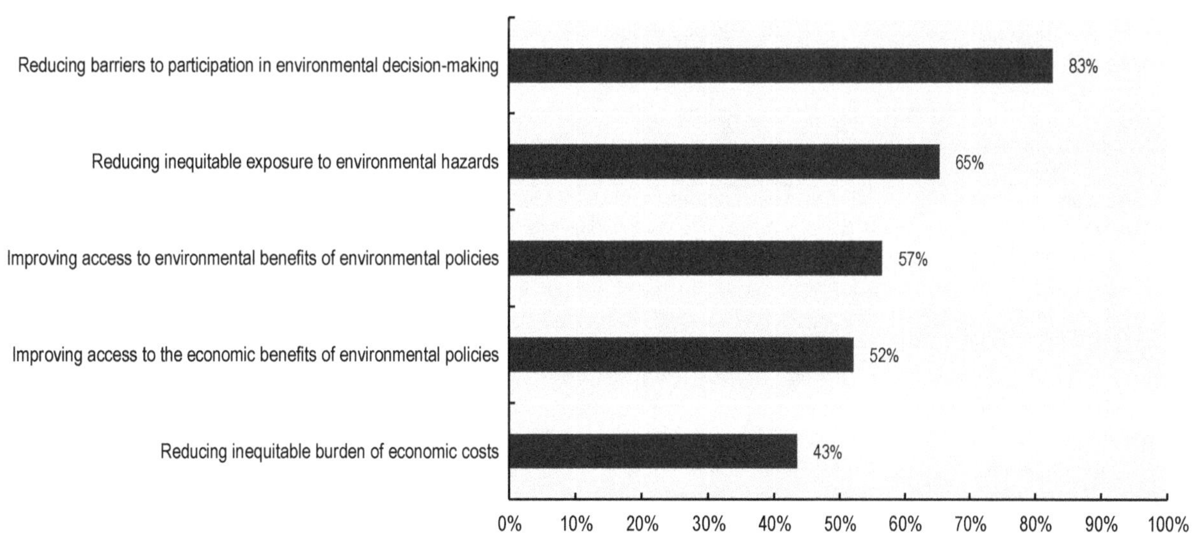


Note: Based on 23 responses. Respondents were asked to select all that apply. The European Commission, Slovak Republic and Spain did not provide a response to this question.
Source: The OECD Environmental Justice Survey.

*Reducing barriers to participation in environmental decision-making*

Exploring the various ways through which countries encourage participation, most countries focus primarily on facilitating public participation in environmental policy processes. Consultations are widespread, with many countries mandating and establishing dedicated mechanisms and tools to engage the public. Examples include dedicated websites (England and Scotland (United Kingdom)), implementation of public comments (Japan) and mandatory consultations when applying for environmental permits (Sweden). Consultations can also assume different forms depending on the context, needs and resources, as Chile's experience with implementing various participatory activities demonstrates (Box 4.6).

## Box 4.6. Varying modalities of participation in Chile

### Participatory implementation of the Escazú Agreement

Following the Early Participation Process, Chile has begun to develop the National Participatory Implementation Plan of Escazú 2024-2030 (PIPE). The Plan addresses five pillars through 56 general actions with a commitment to implementation between 2024 and 2030. Amongst other things, the Plan seeks to address the need to:

- Inform citizens more comprehensively
- Consider children and adolescents in decision-making
- Review the rules for citizen participation in public services
- Participate earlier in the elaboration of public policies
- Train civil servants and citizens on access rights and environmental protection
- Have mechanisms for the exchange of experiences on access right
- Create and update existing information platforms.
- Move towards the protection of personal data.
- Reorganise the work of human rights defenders on environmental issue.
- Promote legal reform to reduce asymmetries in access to justice, including by considering the dynamic burden of proof in procedures for liability for environmental damages.

These actions are reflected in 236 measures from public institutions incorporated into the plan (Table 4.1).

### Table 4.1. Example measures relating to the National Participatory Plan of Escazú 2024-2030 (PIPE)

| Pillar | Examples of relevant measures by Chilean Ministries and other public institutions |
|---|---|
| Access to public environmental information | Creation of new participatory modalities for Indigenous Consultations such as meetings between Indigenous Human Groups and the environment assessment service (measure 162) |
| | Creation of a Science and Technology Information System on Climate Change to make data and scientific knowledge available to the public (measure 16) |
| | Development of internal data protection protocol to help anonymise environmental complaints (measure 205) |
| Access to public participation in environmental decision-making | Update the General Standard of Citizen Participation within the framework law 20,500 (measure 18) |
| Access to justice in environmental matters | Disseminate details on both state and non-state access to justice tools as well as extrajudicial legal proceedings (measure 56) |
| Human rights defenders in environmental matters | Creation of plan to enhance competency of healthcare providers and address access to healthcare for environmental defenders who suffered attacks, intimidation, or threats (measure 82) |
| | Creation of Chilean Protocol on Human Rights Defenders which enables inter-institutional coordination for the protection of human rights defenders (measure 58) |
| Strengthening capacities and cooperation | Train officials on transparency, access rights to information, and accountability in environmental matters (measure 2) |

Source: (Ministerio del Medio Ambiente, 2024[31])

**Consultation of the amendment of Law 19.300**

Citizen consultation is also key in the ongoing process of amending the Law 19.300 on the General Bases of the Environment (1994), which establishes the framework for environmental protection and instruments including Environmental Impact Assessment, in light of new environmental challenges. To ensure meaningful citizen participation, a series of in-person Participatory Dialogues was held across all 16 regions of Chile. The Dialogues, open to all, aimed at engaging as many participants as possible and consisted of two parts: 1) presentation of the proposed amendments to the law; and 2) participatory workshops to gather citizens' opinions. Complementing in-person meetings, an online mailbox was made available. Outcomes of each Dialogue were subsequently published on the Ministry website and presented in a webinar.

**Variety of modalities available can help ensure meaningful participation**

In Chile, a diverse array of citizen participation methods is employed. This is especially important as traditional consultations alone may not reflect the breadth of views in the society due to the presence of selection bias (see Section 2.4.3 in Chapter 2). A variety of methods can help ensure the diversity of perspectives. Modalities such as self-convened town halls can be particularly beneficial in remote areas where the presence of government officials is limited. Similarly, due to potential barriers to participation faced by vulnerable groups such as youth or Indigenous Peoples, devising activities that target them specifically can increase the visibility of their views.

Source: (Ministerio del Medio Ambiente, 2023[32]), (Ministerio del Medio Ambiente, 2023[33]), (Ministerio del Medio Ambiente, n.d.[34]), (Ministerio del Medio Ambiente, n.d.[35]), (Ministerio del Medio Ambiente, 2024[31]), (United Nations, 2024[36]).

Furthermore, some countries engage with the public in the development of major environmental and climate plans and strategies through deliberative processes. Lithuania noted its National Energy and Climate Plan for 2021-2030, developed in close consultations with local and regional stakeholders, associations, and the general public through a series of events and a dedicated online consultation platform.[12] Similarly, in Germany, the Climate Adaptation Dialogue was held in 2023, with online participation (with a dedicated platform for youth aged between 14 and 25) and regional events with samples of randomly chosen participants, to develop the German Strategy for Adaptation to Climate Change under the nationwide climate adaptation law (Federal Ministry for Environment, Nature Conservation and Nuclear Safety, 2023[37]).

Identifying key stakeholders in a strategic, rather than necessarily complete, manner can complement participatory mechanisms to enable the most affected to ensure their views are represented in decision-making processes. In this context, some countries adopt more targeted approaches to engage with specific segments of the population. For instance, Chile, Colombia, Costa Rica, Mexico, New Zealand and Peru highlighted they deploy specific mechanisms for consulting Indigenous Peoples, recognising the unique role of Indigenous Peoples in caring for the environment and the historical legacy of discrimination.

In addition, over half of countries have measures to improve access to information. Many countries have measures in place to ensure transparency and make information available upon request. For instance, Sweden makes applications for permits for activities with the risk of environmental hazards, together with their environmental impact statements, available to the public by default. Scotland ensures access to requested information in the 2004 Environmental Information Regulations (Public Health Scotland, 2023[38]).

Maps and data portals that are used for assessing environmental concerns (see Section 4.2.1) can also serve as a valuable tool for informing the public. For instance, New Zealand's Ministry of Health provides funding for "Environmental Health Intelligence New Zealand", which not only provides data dashboard and information on environmental hazards but also profiles of vulnerable population groups and their regional variabilities, as well as dedicated statistics on Māori environmental health (Environmental Health Intelligence New Zealand, n.d.[39]). Similarly, the Korean Environmental Health Comprehensive Information System provides information on environmental hazards across neighbourhoods, made accessible with the use of icons and images and a range of educational materials (Ministry of Environment, n.d.[40]).

Meanwhile, some of the initiatives focus on actively delivering environmental information to the public. Poland developed the "Air quality in Poland" mobile application which provides air quality information, forecasts, warnings, and maps. Polish citizens can also receive SMS warnings when an alarming level of PM10 is observed. A similar solution is deployed in South Africa, where the South African Air Quality Information System (SAAQIS) is available both online and through a mobile application. The example of South Africa highlights the importance of tailoring tools to the local context; less than one third of citizens have access to computers and mobile phones are important devices for informing citizens about the environmental risks.[13] South Africa also notes that lack of public awareness of environmental challenges constitutes an important barrier to information. Reflecting the role of mainstream media such as television as the key source of information for citizens, South Africa is also exploring a pilot in collaboration with popular television shows, integrating environmental information in the scripts to raise public awareness.

While approaches to removing barriers to information vary from making information available to actively delivering information, these initiatives rarely have a targeted focus for vulnerable communities. The US EPA's Office of Environmental Justice and External Civil Rights' monthly online engagement calls are among a few examples of policy measures directly targeting procedural environmental justice that seeks to inform the vulnerable communities about ongoing policy initiatives (Box 4.7).

### Box 4.7. National Environmental Justice Community Engagement Calls

Monthly National Environmental Justice Community Engagement Calls are held by the US EPA's Office of Environmental Justice and External Civil Rights to meaningfully engage, and better inform the public about the Office's work on environmental justice. Through this form of direct dialogue, the public can provide feedback on the agency's activities as well as participate in "Questions and Answers" sessions and receive information regarding, for example, grant applications or the agency's upcoming programmes. Examples of topics discussed during the calls are:

> *An Overview of new Presidential Executive Orders and Memoranda (2021) related to Environmental Justice*
>
> *EJ Programme Updates, including NEJAC, EJScreen, Collaboration with States and Tribes*
>
> *EJScreen 2.0: What's New in EPA's Environmental Justice Screening Tool*

Its online format can facilitate public engagement, allowing the participation regardless of the place of residence. As the number of participants during a webinar is limited, recordings of all sessions are provided on the EPA's website. Moreover, transcripts of some sessions are published both in English and Spanish, thus enabling access to information for persons with hearing impairment and those with limited English proficiency.

Source: (United States Environmental Protection Agency, n.d.[41]).

Meanwhile, only about one third of countries have policy measures to facilitate access of potentially interested persons to administrative and judicial procedures in environmental matters. New Zealand facilitates not-for-profit organisations' access to public interest litigations in environmental matters through financial assistance provided through a dedicated Environmental Legal Assistance Fund (Ministry for the Environment, 2024[42]). Others indirectly enable access to justice by strengthening enforcement and compliance with environmental legislation by increasing the capacity and knowledge of government officials in environmental law and administrative enforcement. In South Africa, the Environmental Management Inspectorate (EMI) was established to improve monitoring and enforcement in the various segments of the legislations including pollution and coastal management (Department of Forestry, Fisheries and the Environment, n.d.[43]). The Inspectorate is composed of the "Green Scorpions" – local, provincial, and national government officials – who undergo a mandatory training course, including in environmental law.

Although the survey responses generally did not refer to environmental courts and tribunals (ECTs), desk research reveals that about half of countries have established such institutions.[14] Relatedly, several countries also improve access to justice by clustering relevant administrative tribunals, such as urban planning and environment, to streamline the process (OECD and Open Society Foundations, 2016[44]). Contrary to traditional courts which may lack specialised knowledge on environmental matters, ECTs can be staffed with judges who are well-versed in environmental science, increasing their capacity to provide effective access to environmental justice (Robinson, 2012[45]). Moreover, their jurisdictional authority and dedicated resources can enable development of influential jurisprudence (UNEP, 2022[46]). ECTs also often provide legal and technical aid to claimants and have more relaxed procedural requirements and streamlined procedures, thus facilitating effective access to justice (UNEP, 2019[47]).

### *Reducing inequitable exposure to environmental hazards*

Although many countries (65%) have policy measures in place to reduce inequitable exposure to environmental hazards, the majority of the measures cited are targeted at overall improvement of environmental quality. These include amendments to waste management laws (Mexico), environmental assessments (Portugal, South Korea) and permitting for new industrial facilities and landfills (England, Scotland (United Kingdom)). Some countries also highlighted policy mechanisms that advance procedural dimension of environmental justice by strengthening the legal basis for recourse (Scotland, United Kingdom) and improving effective access to remediation for environmental pollution (Japan, South Korea).

Fewer countries have more targeted measures for alleviating the environmental burden for specific groups or regions, although it is important to note that the implementation of targeted measures might reflect historical and pre-existing concerns over inequitable exposures that are more salient. Examples include the US Justice40 Initiative which aims to direct at least 40% of the benefits of certain federal programs (e.g. related to investments in clean energy, remediation and reduction of legacy pollution) to communities burdened by underinvestment and pollution (White House, n.d.[48]). Similarly, the Bipartisan Infrastructure Law requires that 49% of the funds to improve drinking water infrastructure be directed at disadvantaged communities (White House, 2021[49]). Another notable example of environmental justice concerns leading to policy action to address unequal distribution of environmental hazards is the case of "Sacrifice Zones" in Chile (Box 4.8).

**Box 4.8. Addressing environmental injustice in "Sacrifice Zones", Chile**

The term "sacrifice zones" has been used to describe areas where communities live near pollution-intensive industries and suffer the consequences of the various pollutants they generate. The term describes: "a situation of evident environmental injustice, in that the benefits generated by [industry] are diffusely distributed throughout society as a whole, while the environmental costs are borne by people in situations of social and economic vulnerability." (Instituto Nacional de Derechos Humanos, 2011[50]). With focus both on managing the transition of industries and disaggregated impact on communities', Chile's approach also highlights the cross-over between just transition policies and environmental justice.

The finding that 40 children became unwell because of exposure to high levels of arsenic in the air surrounding their school which was positioned next to a large copper refinery raised visibility of the issue of sacrifice zones in Chile. This, and other similar events, gave rise to greater recognition of the intersectionality of environmental rights with various issues – such as health, work, housing, or education – and catalysed a movement which led to Chile's "Environment and Social Recovery Plans" (ESRPs).

In the ESRPs for Huasco, Quintero-Puchuncaví, and Coronel, various ways of addressing sacrifice zones are currently implemented. The Chilean administration categorises these solutions under the headings of air, water, sea, soil, landscape and biodiversity, society, health, and infrastructure. The table below (Table 4.2) provides some examples of these solutions taken from the ESRPs noted by Chile in their response to the survey (Ministerio del Medio Ambiente, Gobierno de Chile, n.d.[51]).

**Table 4.2. Examples of policies in the Chilean Environmental and Social Recovery Plans (ESPRs)**

| | Environmental and Social Recovery Plan |
|---|---|
| Air quality | Update air quality standards (e.g. for sulphur dioxide) |
| | Establish monitoring station to improve the air quality |
| | Develop training programme on air quality and emissions aimed at relevant actors |
| | Create publicly accessible web platform providing access to data from monitoring stations |
| Other Health | Implement programme for surveillance of people's health |
| | Develop closure plan to reclaim landfill space |
| | Develop composting programme to reduce organic waste |
| | Improve waste management of micro, small and medium sized enterprises |
| Social | Develop conservation plans for areas not yet affected by human activity |
| | Develop projects that generate quality public spaces |
| | Clean up waste from industrial park and establish areas for forestation with native species |
| | Regulate entry of new companies which produce dangerous pollutants |

Source: (Ministerio del Medio Ambiente, Gobierno de Chile, n.d.[51]).

While the ESRPs and the broader framework of the Just Socio-Ecological Transition adopted by Chile in recent years provide a solid institutional foundation, challenges remain for their implementation. Improving data collection with the use of screening and mapping tools could facilitate the identification of relevant communities, overburdened by pollution and the design of well-targeted policies. Furthermore, in view of the coal phase-out and carbon tax and their impacts on employment and low-income households, the Just Socio-Ecological Transition is predicated on more comprehensive social assistance programmes (OECD, 2024[52]).

1. In addition, as pointed out in the report of the UN Special Rapporteur on human rights and the environment, important differences exist with regard to the capacity to adapt to the creation of "sacrifice zones" – while for wealthier residents it may be easier to relocate to an area with better environmental quality, low-income residents may lack alternatives and are thus unavoidably compelled to endure the negative health impacts (Office of the United Nations High Commissioner for Human Rights, 2023[53]).

*Improving access to environmental benefits of environmental policies*

Over half of the countries (57%) implement measures aimed at improving access to the environmental benefits of environmental policies. In Sweden, access to environmental benefits is mandated by the Planning and Building Act, which states that "planning, with regard to natural and cultural values, environmental and climate aspects, as well as inter-municipal and regional conditions, must promote, among other things, a socially good living environment that is accessible and useful for all social groups". Across many countries, there is an emphasis on enhancing access to environmental amenities in urban areas. For instance, the German Federal Ministry for the Environment provides support to local authorities to implement a wide-ranging programme to improve quality and access to green and recreational space under its "Urban Nature Master Plan". Similarly, "Environmental Improvement Plan 2023" uses the fund dedicated to addressing regional inequalities in England[15] to create and refurbish green spaces in deprived urban neighbourhoods (Department for Environment, Food and Rural Affairs, 2023[54]). Other examples of policy measures that enhance access to environmental benefits focus on protection of biodiversity (Costa Rica) as well as nature conservation and wildlife rehabilitation projects (Portugal).

*Improving access to economic benefits of environmental policies*

Just over half of countries (52%) have policy measures to improve access to economic benefits of environmental policies. Most measures countries use entail tailoring the design of broader policies that support modernisation and weatherisation of buildings and sustainable transport and mobility. For example, support provided for improving energy efficiency under the Polish "Clean Air Programme" is determined by income thresholds, prioritising less affluent households. Similarly, France has adopted income-based subsidy schemes for facilitating take-up of green technologies and investments in energy efficiency.

A more direct approach to improve access to economic benefits of environmental policy is taken in Costa Rica through its use of payment for ecosystem services programme, in operation since 1997. This programme pays landowners, including Indigenous communities who steward their territories for sustainable management of forests on their lands, contributing to increasing the forest cover and providing sources of employment and income.

*Reducing inequitable burden of economic costs of environmental policies*

Notably, less than half (43%) of countries address the inequitable burden of economic costs of environmental policies, despite the distributive consequences of environmental policy through their impact on income and prices (Vona, 2021[55]). This may reflect the challenges in identifying and considering the implications of environmental policies at the granularity required to inform the policy design to mitigate distributive consequences.

Eight countries included the mention of the concept of just transition which is closely linked to the issue of distribution of economic costs and benefits of environmental policy. For example, the Scottish Government cites their policy document "Just Transition: A Fairer Greener Scotland" which details the need to ensure the costs of the transition to a more environmentally sustainable economy do not overburden those least able to pay. Likewise, the European Commission highlights Just Transition Mechanism under the European Green Deal (Box 4.9). Relatedly, the European Commission has established the Social Climate Fund, explicitly apportioning part of the revenues from carbon pricing towards mitigating distributional impact of environmental policy for the most adversely affected in light of the extension of the emissions trading system (ETS) to transport and building sectors. The funds can be directed towards households facing energy or transport poverty, through support for investments in energy efficiency, renovation of buildings and zero- and low-emission mobility (European Commission, n.d.[56]). These policies may help alleviate the transitional impact, but applying environmental justice lens can complement them by identifying overlooked vulnerabilities and ensure they do not compound the distributive consequences of increasingly stringent environmental policy.

**Box 4.9. Addressing uneven distribution of costs and benefits of environmental policy through just transition strategies – the case of the European Union**

Aiming at addressing uneven social and economic impacts of environmental policy across sectors and communities, just transition have been placed high on policy agendas in recent years. The European Commission's response provides an illustration of how this concept is applied in practice. The Commission's flagship European Green Deal is explicit in its aim to ensure the transition will "leave no one or no region behind".

To this end, Just Transition Mechanism mobilises EUR 55 billion (2021-2027) in the affected regions. The Mechanism consists of three key pillars of: (i) Just Transition Fund, (ii) a dedicated scheme under InvestEU, and (iii) a public sector loan facility with the European Investment Bank.

The largest component of the Mechanism, Just Transition Fund is expected to mobilise around EUR 25.4 billion in investments provided for Member States to support economic diversification and reconversion of the most adversely impacted regions. The fund is directed to address various economic and social impacts of environmental policy based on Member States' Territorial Just Transition Plans and can be used for up- and reskilling, environmental rehabilitation, transforming existing carbon-intensive industries, as well as for social infrastructures (European Commission, 2021[57]).

A number of other tools and non-binding guidance provide the EU Member States with information and knowledge to support the transition to climate neutrality. The Just Transition Platform provides information and guidance on available support measures for the EU territories in transition. It also promotes mutual learning and exchange of knowledge, holding regular events for stakeholders as well as publishing case studies and toolkits. In addition to the sectoral and regional focus of the Just Transition Mechanism, the Council Recommendation of 16 June 2022 on ensuring a fair transition towards climate neutrality draws attention to 'people and households in vulnerable situation' who independently of the green transition face disadvantages in terms of access to employment, education or a decent standard of living, recognising the particular vulnerability of certain populations.

Insofar as just transition seeks to address both the uneven labour market impact of environmental policy and pollution, they also advance environmental justice by reducing inequitable exposure while shielding the vulnerable from the income losses and unemployment.

Source : (European Commission, n.d.[56]), (European Commission, n.d.[58]), (European Commission, n.d.[59]), (European Commission, n.d.[60]), (The Council of the European Union, 2022[61]).

## 4.4. Challenges in assessing and addressing environmental justice concerns

This section summarises the findings on what constitutes barriers to integrating environmental justice into environmental policymaking across countries. The findings are based on the following set of questions:

> *What data or methodological challenges countries face in assessing the risk or exposure of different communities or groups to environmental hazards;*
>
> *What challenges countries face in addressing issues such as inequitable exposure to environmental hazards, inequitable economic burden of environmental policies, or barriers to participating in environmental decision-making.*

### 4.4.1. Data and methodologies

Data and methodological challenges in assessing the risks and exposure of different groups to environmental hazards can be considerable. The survey finds that many countries (65%) face these challenges. The most common challenge across countries is limited data availability, with several countries (Chile, France, Germany, Mexico, Peru the United States) and the European Commission highlighting the need for precise and sufficiently granular environmental, socio-economic and demographic indicators that can be integrated at the same level of disaggregation. Although the availability and resolution of environmental data has been enhanced by technology, including satellite imagery,[16] demographic data tend to be collected at relatively aggregated level (Weigand et al., 2019[62]). While some additional data may be made available through non-state actors, identifying and leveraging these resources can constitute a challenge (France).

There can also be a complete absence of data on specific issues, for example, on the new risks climate change poses to hazardous activities (Sweden), detailed information on exposure scenarios and exposure factors (South Korea) or a comprehensive registry that identifies the local and Indigenous communities (Mexico). Lack of historical data to measure changes over time (Mexico) and infrequent updates of standardised data (Costa Rica) also pose an important challenge. The European Commission also highlights the difficulties in assessing the impact transnational EU policies might have on communities in other countries, noting the negative social and environmental impact its support for biofuels had in other countries under the first Renewable Energy Directive. For instance, assessment of the impacts the current policy of diversifying sources of raw minerals for the twin transition and importing hydrogen might have in other countries remains challenging. Even when data are available, methodological challenges in the use of data can be paramount, particularly with regard to identifying causal linkages and assessing cumulative impacts, as noted by South Korea, Canada and the United States. Relatedly, the Slovak Republic also highlighted the hurdles in analysing the data through an intersectional lens.

### 4.4.2. Capacity and resources

Capacity and resource constraints are pertinent to both data and methodologies and policy implementation across most of the countries. Perhaps reflecting the relative lack of dedicated tools that allow for the integrated analysis of environmental, social and economic data (Section 4.2.1), combined use of data is a notable challenge that is further complicated by the need for improvement in the command of economic analysis to inform policy (France). Constructing an index for assessing environmental justice concerns, for instance requires judgements on the relevant and appropriate variables (Shrestha et al., 2016[63]). In addition, a few countries (Costa Rica, Lithuania and Portugal) highlight the budgetary concerns due to, for instance, high cost of conducting additional studies.

As Germany and Lithuania point out, the lack of conceptual clarity of environmental justice and overall complexity of the issue can pose further challenges on the effective use of resources and capacity. For instance, Lithuania highlights that there is lack of information, methodological guidance and best practices on how the assessment can be integrated in the existing procedures. In a similar vein, the Slovak Republic points to the need to develop a framework for the inclusion and consideration of vulnerable groups in policy-making processes.

Furthermore, capacity and resources also play a pivotal role in the context of monitoring and enforcement for ensuring the effectiveness of environmental policy. This is illustrated by the example of South Africa, where the electricity supply crisis hampers the maintenance and repair of air pollution monitoring devices, impeding the collection of necessary data. Relatedly, as the state's capacity to supply electricity declines, illustrated by frequent power cuts, the quality of air can worsen, due to the surge in reliance on diesel or petrol-run generators, as well as coal or wood combustion (Langerman et al., 2023[64]).

### 4.4.3. Difficulties in reaching the affected communities

While implementing targeted programmes for the most affected communities can be challenging in general as noted by Croatia, there are also locally specific challenges for data collection and policy implementation. For instance, collecting environmental information can incur the risk of facing violence as mentioned by Colombia. Canada and the United States both note that Indigenous Peoples and Tribes often lack resources to engage in consultations, and in the United States, they also face the challenge of leveraging available federal financial resources. Language barriers can also pose significant challenges. As pointed out by Peru, providing translation is key to ensure equitable access to information and participation for Indigenous communities. This is especially challenging in linguistically diverse countries, such as Peru, where 48 indigenous languages are spoken across the country (Base de datos de Pueblos Indígenas u Originarios, Ministerio de Cultura, n.d.[65]). While some are relatively widespread, such as Quechua with almost 4 million speakers, others are spoken by only a few hundred speakers (*ibid*).

### 4.4.4. Co-ordination across different levels of administrations

Another complexity that adds to the challenge is the need to ensure co-ordination across different agencies and departments. Consensus on environmental issues that involve a wide range of stakeholders can be difficult to attain (South Korea). The multi-faceted nature of environmental justice requires a unified vision and strategy to coordinate policy responses across domains, yet different responsibilities and priorities assigned across different ministries and agencies make the implementation challenging in practice (Germany). Similarly, there is a need for simplifying legal and institutional frameworks (Costa Rica). Inadequate co-ordination between multiple departments can also hinder the integration of data from different sectors (Peru) and those collected at the local level (New Zealand).

These issues can also arise at sub-national levels. For instance, Canadian municipalities are under provincial and territorial jurisdiction and federal options for engaging with communities directly on environmental justice issues are limited. This limits the national administrations' understanding of the scope of actions taken by sub-national governments and departments, particularly when the sub-national initiatives do not explicitly state advancing environmental justice as an objective. Similarly, in the United States, certain authorities are delegated to states, which creates challenges for standardising consideration of environmental justice across state and federal level decision-making. This also leads to difficulties in tracking the overall progress to identify areas for further action.

## 4.5. Key insights

Most countries emphasise the procedural aspect of environmental justice, possibly reflecting the influence of international agreements in shaping national approaches to enhance participatory opportunities, and access to information and justice. However, the approaches countries deploy do not appear to specifically focus upon removing barriers for communities for whom meaningful engagement remains a challenge. There are some novel approaches including the use of cultural mediators to engage more effectively with Indigenous communities, that can yield insights for the design and implementation of meaningful engagement. Further research is warranted to understand the extent to which these measures do reduce barriers, and subsequently, improve environmental and social outcomes for the most vulnerable groups.

While countries consider the disproportionate impact of environmental policies, they tend to do so at a relatively aggregated level, such as through a focus on low-income households or the sectoral impact of climate policies. This underscores the scope for applying the inward-looking environmental justice lens to the analysis of differentiated impacts of policies, resulting from the excessive focus on more measurable and quantifiable impacts at the cost of masking less visible impacts. Despite the unequivocal importance and desirability of environmental policies, lack of consideration for their impact on communities may lead to oversight of distinct vulnerabilities.

Despite the variability in approaches, one notable finding of this analysis is that key challenges in advancing environmental justice are often shared across countries. Across many contexts, limited data availability and difficulties in combining different types of data, pose difficulties to informing policies to advance environmental justice. Another significant obstacle is capacity and resource constraints, compounded by the lack of conceptual clarity of environmental justice as well as the difficulties in ensuring national and sub-national efforts add up to contribute towards a unified vision for pursuing environmental justice.

In this context, lessons drawn from the development of a suite of tools, methodologies and approaches to policy measures emanating from across jurisdictions can carry over across different countries. The examples such as the development of screening tools at national and sub-national levels, for instance, can attenuate the challenges of capacity constraints. Complementing these tools that facilitate assessments are approaches of reorienting existing frameworks and laws to consider vulnerabilities of communities. These practices from across countries suggest that there is an important scope for knowledge exchange to address the unifying challenges of advancing environmental justice. Rather than restricting, the value of mutual learning lies in the diversity of approaches across different countries.

## References


Base de datos de Pueblos Indígenas u Originarios, Ministerio de Cultura (n.d.), *Lista de lenguas indígenas u originarias*, https://bdpi.cultura.gob.pe/lenguas (accessed on 23 April 2024). [65]

Butler, B., A. Gripper and N. Linos (2022), "Built and Social Environments, Environmental Justice, and Maternal Pregnancy Complications", *Current Obstetrics and Gynecology Reports*, Vol. 11/3, https://doi.org/10.1007/s13669-022-00339-2. [6]

City of Westminster (2022), *Environmental Justice Measure*, https://www.westminster.gov.uk/about-council/data/environmental-justice-measure (accessed on 23 April 2024). [22]

CONAGEBIO (n.d.), *Protección del conocimiento tradicional*, https://www.conagebio.go.cr/es/node/69 (accessed on 23 April 2024). [30]

Department for Environment, Food and Rural Affairs (2023), *Environment Improvement Plan*, https://assets.publishing.service.gov.uk/government/uploads/system/uploads/attachment_data/file/1168372/environmental-improvement-plan-2023.pdf. [54]

Department for Levelling Up, Housing and Communities (2022), *Levelling Up Parks Fund: Prospectus*, https://www.gov.uk/government/publications/levelling-up-parks-fund-prospectus/levelling-up-parks-fund-prospectus. [73]

Department of Forestry, Fisheries and the Environment (n.d.), *Green Scorpions, Protecting South Africa's future*, https://www.dffe.gov.za/sites/default/files/docs/publications/greenscorpions_newspaperinsert.pdf. [43]

Department of Forestry, Fisheries and the Environment (n.d.), *National Web based Environmental Screening Tool*, https://screening.environment.gov.za/screeningtool/#/pages/welcome (accessed on 23 April 2024). [23]

Ebi, K. and K. Bowen (2023), *Green and blue spaces: crucial for healthy, sustainable urban futures*, https://doi.org/10.1016/S0140-6736(23)00096-X. [70]

Environmental Health Information System (n.d.), *National Environmental Health Survey*, https://www.ehtis.or.kr/cmn/sym/mnu/mpm/62002000/htmlMenuView.do (accessed on 23 April 2024). [25]

Environmental Health Intelligence New Zealand (n.d.), *Monitoring New Zealand's Environmental Health*, https://www.ehinz.ac.nz/ (accessed on 23 April 2024). [39]

European Commission (2022), *National Energy and Climate Action Plan of the Republic of Lithuania for 2021-2030*, https://energy.ec.europa.eu/system/files/2022-08/lt_final_necp_main_en.pdf. [72]

European Commission (2021), *COMMISSION STAFF WORKING DOCUMENT SWD(2021) 452 final*, https://www.google.com/url?sa=t&rct=j&q=&esrc=s&source=web&cd=&cad=rja&uact=8&ved=2ahUKEwjoqoiDzaqFAxWxUqQEHbKiCl4QFnoECBEQAQ&url=https%3A%2F%2Fec.europa.eu%2Fsocial%2FBlobServlet%3FdocId%3D25029%26langId%3Den&usg=AOvVaw0dzymExom7mKU6zM8bnTMU&opi=89978449. [57]

European Commission (n.d.), *About the Just Transition Platform*, https://ec.europa.eu/regional_policy/funding/just-transition-fund/just-transition-platform/about_en (accessed on 23 April 2024). [59]

European Commission (n.d.), *Just Transition Fund*, https://commission.europa.eu/funding-tenders/find-funding/eu-funding-programmes/just-transition-fund_en (accessed on 23 April 2024). [58]

European Commission (n.d.), *Knowledge Repository*, https://ec.europa.eu/regional_policy/funding/just-transition-fund/just-transition-platform/knowledge-repository_en (accessed on 23 April 2024). [60]

European Commission (n.d.), *The Just Transition Mechanism: making sure no one is left behind*, https://commission.europa.eu/strategy-and-policy/priorities-2019-2024/european-green-deal/finance-and-green-deal/just-transition-mechanism_en (accessed on 23 April 2024). [56]

Falanga, R. et al. (2021), “The participation of senior citizens in policy-making: Patterning initiatives in Europe.”, *International Journal of Environmental Research and Public Health*, Vol. 18/1, https://doi.org/10.3390/ijerph18. [69]

Federal Ministry for Environment, Nature Conservation and Nuclear Safety (2023), *Bundesregierung verabschiedet erstes bundesweites Klimaanpassungsgesetz*, https://www.bmuv.de/pressemitteilung/bundesregierung-verabschiedet-erstes-bundesweites-klimaanpassungsgesetz (accessed on 23 April 2024). [37]

Fowlie, M., E. Rubin and R. Walker (2019), “Bringing Satellite-Based Air Quality Estimates Down to Earth”, *AEA Papers and Proceedings*, Vol. 109, https://doi.org/10.1257/pandp.20191064. [68]

Giudice, L. et al. (2021), “Climate change, women’s health, and the role of obstetricians and gynecologists in leadership”, *International Journal of Gynecology and Obstetrics*, Vol. 155/3, https://doi.org/10.1002/ijgo.13958. [5]

Harper, K., T. Steger and R. Filčák (2009), “Environmental justice and Roma communities in Central and Eastern Europe”, *Environmental Policy and Governance*, Vol. 19/4, https://doi.org/10.1002/eet.511. [67]

Instituto Nacional de Derechos Humanos (2011), *Informe Anual 2011, Situación de los Derechos Humanos en Chile*, https://www.indh.cl/wp-content/uploads/2011/12/27555-Informe-Anual-2011-BAJA1.pdf. [50]

Intergovernmental Panel on Climate Change (2023), “IPCC, 2022: Annex II: Glossary”, in *Climate Change 2022 – Impacts, Adaptation and Vulnerability. Contribution of Working Group II to the Sixth Assessment Report of the Intergovernmental Panel on Climate Change*. [26]

International Labour Organization (1989), *C169 - Indigenous and Tribal Peoples Convention, 1989 (No. 169)*, https://www.ilo.org/dyn/normlex/en/f?p=NORMLEXPUB:55:0::NO::P55_TYPE,P55_LANG,P55_DOCUMENT,P55_NODE:REV,en,C169,/Document (accessed on 23 April 2024). [27]

L'Institut national de la statistique et des études économiques (2016), *Ethnic-based statistics*, https://www.insee.fr/en/information/2388586 (accessed on 23 April 2024). [75]

Landrigan, P., V. Rauh and M. Galvez (2010), "Environmental justice and the health of children", *Mount Sinai Journal of Medicine*, Vol. 77/2, https://doi.org/10.1002/msj.20173. [3]

Langerman, K. et al. (2023), *South Africa's electricity disaster is an air quality disaster, too*, https://doi.org/10.17159/caj/2023/33/1.15799. [64]

Massimo, F. and P. Mannucci (2018), "Mitigation of air pollution by greenness: A narrative review", *European Journal of Internal Medicine*, Vol. 55, https://doi.org/10.1016/j.ejim.2018.06.021. [4]

Mathew, S. et al. (2023), "Environmental health injustice and culturally appropriate opportunities in remote Australia", *The Journal of Climate Change and Health*, Vol. 14, https://doi.org/10.1016/j.joclim.2023.100281. [1]

McGregor, D., S. Whitaker and M. Sritharan (2020), *Indigenous environmental justice and sustainability*, https://doi.org/10.1016/j.cosust.2020.01.007. [66]

Ministério da Igualdade Racial, Governo do Brasil (2023), *Anielle Franco anuncia criação de Comitê de Monitoramento da Amazônia Negra e Enfrentamento ao Racismo Ambiental*, https://www.gov.br/igualdaderacial/pt-br/assuntos/copy2_of_noticias/anielle-franco-anuncia-criacao-de-comite-de-monitoramento-da-amazonia-negra-e-enfrentamento-ao-racismo-ambiental (accessed on 23 April 2024). [8]

Ministerio del Medio Ambiente (2024), *Plan Nacional de Implementación Participativa del Acuerdo de Escazú 2024-2030*, https://mma.gob.cl/wp-content/uploads/2024/04/Plan-Nacional-de-implementacion-participativa-del-Acuerdo-de-Escazu-Chile-2024-2030.pdf (accessed on 13 May 2024). [31]

Ministerio del Medio Ambiente (2023), *Informe proceso de participación temprana para la elaboración del plan de implementación participativa del Acuerdo de Escazú. Identificación y Análisis de Brechas y Propuestas de Medidas*, https://consultasciudadanas.mma.gob.cl/storage/records/mRUmlOP9CwB0dB2dUfxprco1gPBWWl3QDEYbmYSD.pdf. [32]

Ministerio del Medio Ambiente (2023), *Ministerio del Medio Ambiente invita a realizar Cabildos Autoconvocados por Escazú*, https://mma.gob.cl/ministerio-del-medio-ambiente-invita-a-realizar-cabildos-autoconvocados-por-escazu/ (accessed on 23 April 2024). [33]

Ministerio del Medio Ambiente (n.d.), *Diálogos participativos*, https://mma.gob.cl/dialogos-participativos/#agenda (accessed on 23 April 2024). [35]

Ministerio del Medio Ambiente (n.d.), *Escazú en Chile*, https://mma.gob.cl/escazu-en-chile/#pipe (accessed on 23 April 2024). [34]

Ministerio del Medio Ambiente, Gobierno de Chile (n.d.), *Programa para la Recuperación Ambiental y Social*, https://pras.mma.gob.cl/ (accessed on 23 April 2024). [51]

Ministry for the Environment (2024), *Environmental Legal Assistance Fund*, https://environment.govt.nz/what-you-can-do/funding/environmental-legal-assistance-fund/ (accessed on 23 April 2024). [42]

Ministry of Environment (n.d.), *Environmental Health Comprehensive Information System*, https://www.ehtis.or.kr/cmn/main/main.do (accessed on 23 April 2024). [40]

Ministry of Justice and Peace (2018), *Poder Ejecutivo Decretos N° 40932 - MP - MJP*, https://www.conagebio.go.cr/sites/default/files/2021-10/Mecanismo-de-Consulta.pdf. [28]

Ministry of the Environment, Government of Japan (n.d.), *Japan Environment and Children's Study*, https://www.env.go.jp/chemi/ceh/en/about/outline.html (accessed on 23 April 2024). [24]

Natural England (2021), *Green Infrastructure*, https://designatedsites.naturalengland.org.uk/GreenInfrastructure/Map.aspx (accessed on 23 April 2024). [12]

Naturally Birmingham (n.d.), *Measuring Environmental Justice in Birmingham*, https://naturallybirmingham.org/environmental-justice/ (accessed on 23 April 2024). [18]

OECD (2024), *OECD Environmental Performance Reviews: Chile 2024*, OECD Environmental Performance Reviews, OECD Publishing, Paris, https://doi.org/10.1787/5bc65d36-en. [52]

OECD (2023), *OECD Environmental Performance Reviews: Costa Rica 2023*, OECD Environmental Performance Reviews, OECD Publishing, Paris, https://doi.org/10.1787/ec94fd4e-en. [29]

OECD (2023), *OECD Environmental Performance Reviews: United States 2023*, OECD Environmental Performance Reviews, OECD Publishing, Paris, https://doi.org/10.1787/47675117-en. [16]

OECD and Open Society Foundations (2016), *Leveraging the SDGs for Inclusive Growth: Delivering Access to Justice for All*, https://www.oecd.org/gov/delivering-access-to-justice-for-all.pdf. [44]

Office of the United Nations High Commissioner for Human Rights (2023), *Statement at the conclusion of country visit to Chile*, https://www.ohchr.org/sites/default/files/documents/issues/environment/srenvironment/eom-statement-Chile-12-May-2023-EN.pdf. [53]

OHCHR (2021), *USA: Environmental racism in "Cancer Alley" must end – experts*, https://www.ohchr.org/en/press-releases/2021/03/usa-environmental-racism-cancer-alley-must-end-experts?LangID=E&NewsID=26824 (accessed on 23 April 2024). [10]

Public Health Scotland (2023), *Freedom of Information (FOI) and Environmental Information Regulation (EIR) requests*, https://publichealthscotland.scot/contact-us/freedom-of-information-foi-and-environmental-information-regulation-eir-requests/ (accessed on 23 April 2024). [38]

Robinson, N. (2012), "Ensuring Access to Justice Through Environmental Courts", *Pace Environmental Law Review*, Vol. 29/2, https://doi.org/10.58948/0738-6206.1691. [45]

Secretaria de Comunicação Social, Governo do Brasil (2024), *O que é racismo ambiental e de que forma ele impacta populações mais vulneráveis*, https://www.gov.br/secom/pt-br/fatos/brasil-contra-fake/noticias/2023/3/o-que-e-racismo-ambiental-e-de-que-forma-impacta-populacoes-mais-vulneraveis (accessed on 23 April 2024). [7]

Senate Department for Urban Mobility, Transport, Climate Action and the Environment (n.d.), *Environmental Justice*, https://www.berlin.de/sen/uvk/en/environment/sustainability/environmental-justice/ (accessed on 23 April 2024). [20]

Shrestha, R. et al. (2016), "Environmental health related socio-spatial inequalities: Identifying "hotspots" of environmental burdens and social vulnerability", *International Journal of Environmental Research and Public Health*, Vol. 13/7, https://doi.org/10.3390/ijerph13070691. [63]

Simoni, M. et al. (2015), "Adverse effects of outdoor pollution in the elderly.", *Journal of Thoracic Disease*, Vol. 7/1, https://doi.org/10.3978/j.issn.2072-1439.2014.12.10. [2]

State of Berlin (n.d.), *Environmental Justice Berlin*, https://www.berlin.de/umweltatlas/en/human/environmental-justice/ (accessed on 23 April 2024). [19]

Statistics South Africa (2022), *General Household Survey, 2021*, https://www.statssa.gov.za/publications/P0318/P03182021.pdf. [74]

Statistics South Africa (2017), *Poverty Trends in South Africa, An examination of absolute poverty between 2006 and 2015*, https://www.statssa.gov.za/publications/Report-03-10-06/Report-03-10-062015.pdf. [71]

The Council of the European Union (2022), *Council Recommendation of 16 June 2022 on ensuring a fair transition towards climate neutrality 2022/C 243/04*, https://eur-lex.europa.eu/legal-content/EN/TXT/PDF/?uri=CELEX:32022H0627(04). [61]

The Scottish Government (2015), *Flood Disadvantage - Scotland*, https://spatialdata.gov.scot/geonetwork/srv/api/records/a23cd103-7381-47e9-841d-083c9aef171d (accessed on 23 April 2024). [11]

The Scottish Government (2015), *Mapping Flood Disadvantage in Scotland 2015: Main Report*, https://www.gov.scot/binaries/content/documents/govscot/publications/research-and-analysis/2015/12/mapping-flood-disadvantage-scotland-2015-main-report/documents/00490788-pdf/00490788-pdf/govscot%3Adocument/00490788.pdf. [13]

The Scottish Government (n.d.), *Mapping Flood Disadvantage in Scotland 2015*, https://www.arcgis.com/home/webmap/viewer.html?webmap=2061e4a5ba134fe3ba3afb58de2c3079&extent=-3.4101,55.8703,-2.903,56.0293 (accessed on 23 April 2024). [14]

UNEP (2022), *Environmental Courts and Tribunals – 2021: A Guide for Policy Makers.*, https://wedocs.unep.org/20.500.11822/40309. [46]

UNEP (2019), *Environmental Rule of Law: First Global Report*, https://wedocs.unep.org/bitstream/handle/20.500.11822/27279/Environmental_rule_of_law.pdf?sequence=1&isAllowed=y. [47]

United Nations (2024), *Third meeting of the Conference of the Parties to the Escazú Agreement*, https://acuerdodeescazu.cepal.org/cop3/en/news/cop-3-escazu-agreement-reinforces-commitment-recognize-protect-and-promote-all-rights-human (accessed on 13 May 2024). [36]

United States Environmental Protection Agency (n.d.), *EJScreen: Environmental Justice Screening and Mapping Tool*, https://www.epa.gov/ejscreen (accessed on 23 April 2024). [17]

United States Environmental Protection Agency (n.d.), *National Environmental Justice Community Engagement Calls*, https://www.epa.gov/environmentaljustice/national-environmental-justice-community-engagement-calls (accessed on 23 April 2024). [41]

United States Environmental Protection Agency (n.d.), *What is EJScreen?*, https://www.epa.gov/ejscreen/what-ejscreen (accessed on 23 April 2024). [15]

Vona, F. (2021), “Managing the distributional effects of environmental and climate policies: The narrow path for a triple dividend”, *OECD Environment Working Papers* 188. [55]

Walker, G. (2012), *Environmental Justice: Concepts, Evidence and Politics*, https://doi.org/10.4324/9780203610671. [9]

Weigand, M. et al. (2019), *Remote sensing in environmental justice research-a review*, https://doi.org/10.3390/ijgi8010020. [62]

Westminster City Council (2022), *Westminster's Environmental Justice Measure*, https://storymaps.arcgis.com/stories/3f7bf2a160e047748e2526b3f2536902 (accessed on 23 April 2024). [21]

White House (2021), *The Bipartisan Infrastructure Law Advances Environmental Justice*, https://www.whitehouse.gov/briefing-room/statements-releases/2021/11/16/the-bipartisan-infrastructure-law-advances-environmental-justice/ (accessed on 23 April 2024). [49]

White House (n.d.), *Justice40*, https://www.whitehouse.gov/environmentaljustice/justice40/ (accessed on 23 April 2024). [48]

## Notes

[1] Their vulnerabilities may also be compounded by their relative lack of access and agency to influence decision-making processes. For instance, children and youth under the voting age may have less opportunities to participate in decision-making, while the elderly with health challenges may face difficulties in exercising their rights fully (Falanga et al., 2021[69]).

[2] Furthermore, in some countries, authorities are prohibited to gather certain types of data, for example data on race and ethnicity in France (L'Institut national de la statistique et des études économiques, 2016[75]).

[3] Although the Black Africans represent over 80% of the country's population, in 2015 64% of them lived in poverty, i.e. living below the upper-bound poverty line. For comparison, only 1% of the white population

lived in poverty in 2015, possibly reflecting the historical legacy of apartheid (Statistics South Africa, 2017[71]).

[4] Roma communities' choices in residence as well as their mobility can be severely limited in practice. For instance, many settlements of Roma communities are found to coincide with contaminated post-industrial sites in Central and Eastern Europe (Harper, Steger and Filčák, 2009[67]).

[5] These countries are Canada, Colombia, Croatia, England (United Kingdom), France, Lithuania, Mexico, Scotland (United Kingdom), South Africa, South Korea, Spain, United States.

[6] These countries are Costa Rica, Estonia, Germany and Peru.

[7] All respondents in the "legal" group reported having or developing such tools, followed by 80% in the "initiatives or policies" group, 67% in the "added protection and safeguards" and finally, only 50% in the "guarantee of rights" group.

[8] Natural England is an executive non-departmental public body, funded by Department for Environment, Food and Rural Affairs in the United Kingdom.

[9] Green and blue spaces refer to a set of infrastructure and amenities such as parks and forests (green) as well as rivers and lakes (blue) that are found to impact health and well-being of the communities (Ebi and Bowen, 2023[70]).

[10] These tools are identified in complementary desk research and were not part of the response from Germany and England.

[11] A distinct Indigenous environmental justice framework points to the need to include Indigenous perspectives' as they provide a unique view of justice, grounded in their experiences, knowledge systems and governance structures. See (McGregor, Whitaker and Sritharan, 2020[66]) for an overview.

[12] See (European Commission, 2022[72]) for a detailed discussion of the processes of public consultations and the subsequent outcomes, which includes a set of proposals incorporated in the alternative policy measures.

[13] In 2021 only 27.3% of South African households owned one or more computers compared to 87.7% who owned televisions. Moreover, the role of mobile devices is key given that they constitute the primary source of access to the Internet. However, access to these resources varies significantly across metropolitan, urban, and rural areas (Statistics South Africa, 2022[74]).

[14] Authors' own calculations based on (UNEP, 2022[46]). In 2021, the following countries had operational ECTs: Australia, Canada, Chile, France, Germany, Japan, New Zealand, Peru, Republic of Korea, South Africa, Spain, Sweden, United Kingdom, United States (*ibid*).

[15] Levelling Up Parks Fund uses the Index of Multiple Deprivation to identify the neighbourhoods most in need of higher quality green space and allocate funding to local authorities (Department for Levelling Up, Housing and Communities, 2022[73]).

[16] While remote sensing data from satellite imagery can aid analysis, there remains challenges including prediction errors (Fowlie, Rubin and Walker, 2019[68]). It can also only detect environmental harms and benefits that can respond to electromagnetic radiation (Weigand et al., 2019[62]).

# Annex A. OECD Environmental Justice Survey

This annex contains the survey which was sent out to OECD member countries, the European Commission and several non-member countries[1] between September 2023 and February 2024, with the purpose to scan national approaches to identify, analyse, and address environmental justice concerns. To facilitate the response the questionnaire was made available in English, French and Spanish.

[1] The survey was sent out to the following countries (countries which provided the response are marked with a *): Argentina, Australia, Austria, Belgium, Brazil, Canada*, Chile*, Colombia*, Costa Rica*, Croatia*, Czechia, Denmark, Estonia*, Finland, France*, Germany*, Greece, Hungary, Iceland, Indonesia, Ireland, Israel, Italy, Japan*, Korea*, Latvia, Lithuania*, Luxembourg, Mexico*, the Netherlands, New Zealand*, Norway, Peru*, Poland*, Portugal*, Slovak Republic*, Slovenia, South Africa*, Spain*, Sweden*, Switzerland*, Türkiye*, the United Kingdom* (where separate responses were received from England and Scotland), and the United States*.

**SECTION 1: Approaches to environmental justice**

This section aims to obtain an understanding of how governments approach environmental justice and how these concerns are reflected in corresponding strategies, policies, plans, or laws. It also seeks to explore how governments identify communities or groups, which are commonly most at risk of experiencing environmental justice concerns.

| | |
|---|---|
| 1. If the concept of environmental justice is used by your administration (government, ministry, agency), how is it defined?<br><br>If the concept is not used, please describe what terminology is used when referring to issues such as:<br>• a group or community's distinct vulnerability to environmental impacts (e.g. due to their level of income, ethnic background, age, health conditions);<br>• inequitable exposure to environmental hazards (e.g. due to the concentration of some communities in certain geographic areas or employment sectors);<br>• inequitable economic burden of environmental policies on communities at risk;<br>• barriers to participation in environmental decision-making, particularly for persons from communities or vulnerable groups at risk. | Please specify: |
| 2. Has your administration set out objectives that fall under the scope of environmental justice as defined in question 1?<br><br>Examples may include:<br>• identifying, analysing, or addressing existing inequalities in the exposure of different communities or groups to environmental hazards;<br>• identifying, analysing, or addressing potential inequitable impacts of proposed or existing environmental programmes, policies, regulations on communities or groups at risk (e.g. measures to offset economic costs of environmental policies);<br>• facilitating public participation in environmental policy processes, particularly for persons from communities or groups at risk. | ☐ Yes. Please elaborate and share relevant sources: ___<br>☐ No |
| 3. If you have such objectives, do you have dedicated strategies, policies, plans, or laws for their implementation? | ☐ Yes (please share relevant sources)<br>☐ No |
| 4. In your administration, do you identify communities or groups at risks?<br><br>Such communities or groups may, due to their social or economic circumstances, face:<br>• inequitable exposure to environmental hazards and to the costs of environmental policies;<br>• unequal access to environmental amenities and the benefits of environmental policies;<br>• limited access to environmental information and participation in related policy processes. | ☐ Yes, we identify communities or groups that may be particularly vulnerable in policy analysis or decision-making:<br>a) ☐ Yes, albeit in a general context<br>b) ☐ Yes, in environmental policy analysis or decision-making<br>☐ Yes, but only informally at an operational level<br>☐ No such communities or groups are identified<br>☐ Other<br><br>If available, please provide reference to related documents. |

5. If the answer to the previous question is "yes", which of the following characteristics do you consider as relevant to identify communities or groups that may be particularly at risk in the context of your jurisdiction? If possible, please specify the kinds of data and sources that are used to inform this analysis. Please select all that apply.

| Indicator | Examples of data and sources (please specify) |
|---|---|
| ☐ Lack of access to key public services (e.g. health care, education, clean water, public transport, public safety) | |

| | |
|---|---|
| ☐ Lack of access to environmental amenities (e.g. parks, safe drinking water) | |
| ☐ Health and disability | |
| ☐ Indigenous populations | |
| ☐ Immigration/migrant status | |
| ☐ Ethnicity or race | |
| ☐ Occupational sector | |
| ☐ Level of income | |
| ☐ Household composition (e.g. single-parent, multi-generation) | |
| ☐ Residential ownership status (e.g. homeowner, renter, social housing resident) | |
| ☐ Gender | |
| ☐ Level of education | |
| ☐ Age | |
| ☐ Minority language | |
| ☐ National origin | |
| ☐ Other (please specify): ___ | |
| 6. Are there regions where certain communities or groups may be particularly exposed to environmental justice concerns as defined by your administration in question 1? | ☐ Yes. Please specify: ____<br>☐ No, we don't target specific regions |
| **SECTION 2: Assessment and data**<br>This section looks at the assessment of environmental hazards and risks and exposure to them. It examines the data, tools, and methods that governments have at their disposal to determine the nature and the distribution of hazards and risks across the general population within their respective jurisdictions. | |
| 7. At what stages of the environmental policy process do you conduct assessments of environmental hazards and risks? Please select all that apply and where possible please complement with additional information and relevant documents. | ☐ Legislation / rulemaking<br>☐ Permitting<br>☐ Monitoring<br>☐ Enforcement<br>☐ Evaluation<br>☐ Other. Please specify: ___ |
| 8. When conducting risk assessments or other types of analysis of environmental hazards (e.g. hazardous waste, air and water pollution), does this include a focus on whether communities or groups at risk are or are likely to be disproportionately exposed or impacted? | ☐ Yes, we always assess if some communities or groups are or are likely to be disproportionately exposed<br>☐ Sometimes, but not systematically<br>If so, what are the criteria for such an assessment to be carried out?<br>Please specify: ___<br>☐ No, we never assess the exposure of a particular community but only for the population in general |
| 9. What data or methodological challenges do you face in assessing the risk or exposure of different communities or groups to environmental hazards? | Please specify: ___ |
| 10. Are qualitative data and methods considered in your assessments of the risk or exposure to environmental hazards? | ☐ Yes. Please specify what data and methods are used and how: ___<br>☐ No, we do not consider qualitative data and methods |
| 11. Do you have specific tools (e.g. interactive maps) that allow decision-makers to combine data and information on environmental, social and economic variables? | ☐ Yes. Please specify and share relevant links: ___<br>☐ No, but we are in the process of developing such tools: ___<br>☐ No, we do not have such tools |
| 12. How are risk assessments and other types of quantitative analysis as well as the results from these analyses, used to inform policy, regulations, legislation, or public outreach to address environmental justice concerns as defined by your administration in question 1? | Please specify: ___ |

| **SECTION 3: Environmental justice implications of policy measures**<br>This section focuses on measures that can address environmental justice concerns. Examples include measures that address inequitable exposure of communities or groups at risk to environmental hazards, improve their access to environmental amenities, mitigate disproportionate costs associated with environmental policies, and facilitate their public engagement and participation in policy processes. | |
|---|---|
| 13. When designing or implementing new environmental laws, regulations, policies, plans or programmes, do you explicitly identify or consider the potential impact of these policies on communities or groups at risk? | ☐ Yes, always. Please specify: ___<br>☐ Sometimes. Please specify: ___<br>☐ No, never |
| 14. If the answer to the previous question is yes, are any communities or groups given particular attention? | ☐ Yes. Please elaborate the characteristics of these communities or groups: ____<br>☐ Sometimes. Please specify: ___<br>☐ No, never |
| 15. What laws, regulations, policies, plans or programmes have been put in place specifically to address environmental justice concerns?<br><br>Some examples of such measures are provided but others can be added. Please select all that apply and where possible please complement with additional information and relevant documents. | Measures aimed at reducing, avoiding or offsetting:<br>☐ Inequitable exposure to environmental hazards (e.g. provisions and criteria in zoning laws, hazardous waste and landfill site permitting, land use planning regulations): ___<br>☐ Inequitable burden of the economic costs of environmental policies (e.g. higher commuting costs due to fossil fuel charges, increased housing prices following a clean-up of polluting activities): ___<br>☐ The barriers to participation in environmental decision-making processes (e.g. public consultations, citizen panels), particularly those faced by persons from communities or groups at risk: ___<br><br>Measures aimed at improving equitable access to:<br>☐ The environmental benefits of environmental policies (e.g. green spaces): ___<br>☐ The economic benefits of environmental policies (e.g. subsidies to climate-resilient housing): ___<br><br>Other<br>☐ Please specify: ___ |
| 16. If you have measures in place aiming to improve public engagement and participation, particularly for persons from communities or groups at risk, can you provide examples of how this engagement informed any regulations, policies, plans or programmes put in place? | Examples of the impact from measures aimed at:<br>☐ Increasing access to environmental information (including information related to human health): ___<br>☐ Facilitating public participation in environmental policy processes: ___<br>☐ Facilitating the access of potentially interested persons to administrative and judicial procedures regarding alleged violations of environmental laws and regulations: ___<br>☐ Other (please specify): ___ |
| 17. Do you allocate a share of revenues of environmental taxes, fees and charges to mitigate economic burdens on communities or groups at risk? | ☐ Yes, a revenue recycling system is in place. Please describe: ____<br>☐ Yes, compensation is done through the general budget<br>☐ No, there is no such system in place |
| 18. What are the challenges you face in addressing issues such as inequitable exposure to environmental hazards, inequitable economic burden of environmental policies, or barriers to participating in environmental decision-making? | Please describe: |
| **Further information** | |
| 19. We are collecting case studies of measures that have successfully identified, analysed or addressed environmental justice concerns. Is there an example from your jurisdiction that you could share? | |
| 20. Do you have any additional comments? | |
| **THANK YOU** | |

www.ingramcontent.com/pod-product-compliance
Lightning Source LLC
Chambersburg PA
CBHW061223240926
51846CB00006B/1328
*9789264509832*